200 chocolate

hamlyn | all colour cookbook

200 chocolate recipes

Felicity Barnum-Bobb

An Hachette Livre UK company
www.hachettelivre.co.uk

First published in Great Britain in 2008 by Hamlyn,
a division of Octopus Publishing Group Ltd
2–4 Heron Quays, London E14 4JP
www.octopusbooks.co.uk

ISBN: 978-0-600-61822-5

A CIP catalogue record for this book is available from the
British Library

Printed and bound in China

1 2 3 4 5 6 7 8 9 10

Both metric and imperial measurements have been given
in all recipes. Use one set of measurements only, and not
a mixture of both.

Standard level spoon measurements are used in all recipes.
1 tablespoon = one 15 ml spoon
1 teaspoon = one 5 ml spoon

Ovens should be preheated to the specified temperature
– if using a fan-assisted oven, follow the manufacturer's
instructions for adjusting the time and the temperature.

In this book, instructions apply to a standard 900 watt
microwave, but the precise wattage is also given where
appropriate. Always refer to the manufacturer's guidelines
before using your microwave.

Medium eggs should be used unless otherwise stated.

The Department of Health advises that eggs should not be
consumed raw. This book contains some dishes made with
raw or lightly cooked eggs. It is prudent for vulnerable
people such as pregnant and nursing mothers, invalids, the
elderly, babies and young children to avoid uncooked or
lightly cooked dishes made with eggs. Once prepared, these
dishes should be kept refrigerated and used promptly.

This book includes dishes made with nuts and nut
derivatives. It is advisable for those with known allergic
reactions to nuts and nut derivatives, and potentially
vulnerable people such as those mentioned above, to avoid
dishes made with nuts and nut oils. Check the labels of pre-
prepared items for the possible inclusion of nut derivatives.

contents

introduction

introduction

We all know that chocolate is 'naughty', yet we still love it. Why? Firstly, it contains sugar, which many of us crave. Like any other sweet food, chocolate stimulates the release of endorphins, natural body hormones that generate feelings of pleasure and wellbeing.

General sweetness aside, there are also various chemical elements specific to chocolate that may help stimulate cravings. Many women report chocolate cravings when premenstrual. This is possibly because chocolate contains magnesium, a shortage of which can exacerbate premenstrual tension. Similar cravings during pregnancy could indicate mild anaemia, which chocolate's iron content may help to cure. Central nervous system stimulants, such as caffeine, are also present in small amounts. These have a mild effect on alertness, as we know from drinking coffee. Another mild stimulant present in chocolate is theobromine, which relaxes the smooth muscles in the lining of the lung.

Chocolate also makes us feel good by interacting with our brain, affecting its neurotransmitter network. Neurotransmitters, the brain's chemical messengers, work by transporting electrical signals between nerve cells. These signals cause changes in our sensations and emotions. Chocolate contains the chemical tryptophan, which is a natural 'love drug' that the brain uses to make the neurotransmitter serotonin. High levels of serotonin can produce feelings of elation, even ecstasy. Current studies of psychoactive drugs show that addiction is associated with the formation and reinforcement of unusual neurotransmitter pathways in the brain. So it is just possible that with every chocolate 'hit' your brain is gradually 'rewired' in order to make you love chocolate more and more!

But could chocolate actually be good for health? Scientists have suggested that the chemicals called flavonoids that chocolate contains might help fight heart disease, by thinning the blood and helping to prevent clotting. Researchers at Harvard University have carried out experiments that suggest that if you eat chocolate 3 times a month

you will live almost a year longer than those who forego such sweet temptation. Sadly, it is not all good news – the Harvard research also suggests that people who eat too much chocolate have a lower life expectancy. Chocolate's high fat content means that excess indulgence can contribute to obesity, leading to an increased risk of heart disease.

It looks as if the old adage of 'everything in moderation' holds. If you cannot resist, stick to dark chocolate, which is higher in cocoa solids than milk chocolate and increases levels of HDL, a type of cholesterol that helps prevent fat clogging up arteries.

types of chocolate

When you buy plain or milk chocolate, remember that the higher the percentage of cocoa solids, the purer the chocolate flavour.

plain chocolate

This is the best type of chocolate to use for cooking. The darkest plain chocolate contains 70–80 per cent cocoa solids and has an intensely chocolaty flavour because of its lower sugar content. I recommend using plain chocolate with 50–60 per cent cocoa solids for most recipes in this book, because it is rich and dark without being too strong. It has a dense, chocolaty flavour and is a good all-rounder. This type of chocolate melts well to a smooth, glossy texture and retains its full flavour. Less expensive brands of plain chocolate contain 30–40 per cent cocoa solids and are best avoided.

Make the most of the exciting range of flavoured plain dark chocolates now available to add variety to these recipes. Flavours include orange, spice, cranberry, cherry, butterscotch, coffee and mint.

milk chocolate

This is considerably sweeter than plain chocolate and has added milk, sugar and flavourings, such as vanilla. It contains 20–30 per cent cocoa solids. The higher the cocoa solids content, the better the flavour will be. It is always a favourite with children.

white chocolate

This contains no solids and instead is made with cocoa butter (the edible fat extracted from the beans during processing), milk, sugar and flavouring. The more expensive brands give the best flavour. Vanilla-flavoured white chocolate is a delicious variation.

cocoa powder

This by-product of the processing method has a strong, bitter flavour. Good for intensifying the flavour of chocolate, it should always be cooked and needs additional sweetening.

chocolate-flavoured cake covering

Usually sold alongside the baking products in supermarkets, this is an imitation chocolate-flavoured bar of sugar, vegetable oils and flavourings. It is best avoided, unless you want to make cheap large chocolate curls quickly

(see page 12). The higher fat content means the curls hold together well, but they won't taste good. An option would be to use one-quarter cake covering mixed with three-quarters good-quality milk or plain chocolate.

how to melt chocolate

Chocolate is delicate when heated, so take care. Gentle heat and minimal stirring are the key to success. Butter, cream, milk and liqueur can be melted with chocolate by any of the methods below; stir a couple of times while melting to help combine the ingredients.

on the hob

Break the chocolate into pieces and put them in a heatproof bowl. Rest the bowl over a pan, one-third filled with water, making sure that the base of the bowl cannot come in contact with the water. Gently heat so the water is simmering. Don't stir the chocolate until it looks melted, then stir a couple of times until smooth. Overstirring will ruin the texture. It is crucial that no water, such as steam from the pan, gets into the bowl while the chocolate is melting, as this will make it solidify. Turn off the heat and either use immediately or leave the chocolate in the bowl over the pan, to remain warm until needed.

in the microwave

This is a very easy way to melt chocolate, as long as you are cautious. Because of its high sugar content, chocolate will burn very easily.

How long it takes to melt depends on the quantity of chocolate. The chocolate holds its shape even when completely melted, so you will only know if it is ready by trying to stir it.

Put 100 g (3½ oz) broken chocolate pieces into a heatproof bowl and microwave on medium (600 watt) for 1 minute; stir and if not softened cook for another 30 seconds, then stir and cook for a further 30 seconds.

For a smaller quantity, heat for 30 seconds initially. Larger quantities are probably best melted on the hob or in the oven.

in the oven

This is a good method if you have a solid-fuel cooker that is on all the time. Put the chocolate in a small ovenproof bowl or dish and leave the bowl in a low oven, 110°C (225°F), Gas Mark ¼, checking frequently. Alternatively, put it in an oven that has been switched off after being used for baking.

sterilizing jars

This is a crucial stage of preparing chocolate spreads (see page 128), as the jars need to be spotlessly clean to guarantee the spread will keep. You can wash the jars in the dishwasher, or alternatively wash them in hot soapy water and dry them off on the lowest setting in the oven for about 15 minutes. The third method is to quarter-fill 4 jars with water. Position on a microwave turntable and microwave on high (900 watt) for 5 minutes, until the water is boiling. Use oven gloves to

remove the jars, pour out the water and drain upturned on kitchen paper. Add the warm chocolate spread to the still warm jars.

equipment

To make these recipes, a few bowls, a large measuring jug, a sieve, a wooden spoon and a muffin tray will suffice. A food processor, blender or mixer, particularly a free-standing one, will help save time. Use at a low speed to avoid beating the mixture to a pulp. Perfect for muffin-making, a food processor will gently combine dry and wet ingredients without overmixing and you won't need to sieve the flour.

To save time, use a microwave to melt the butter – 30 seconds on high (900 watt) and it will be softened enough to use. A microwave is also the fastest means of melting chocolate (see above). Use a food processor or coffee grinder to chop nuts speedily.

secrets of successful baking

Successful baking requires the use of precise measurements and temperatures. Here are some ways of improving accuracy, as well as a few general baking tips:

• Invest in a set of cook's measuring spoons. Household spoons vary greatly in size, so results are not consistent.

• Use digital scales, if possible, as these are the most accurate.

• Check liquid measurements in a jug at eye level, or use scales if you have the digital type that measures liquids too.

• Butter should always be used softened, unless otherwise stated.

• When folding a mixture, always use a metal spoon and make gentle cutting and folding movements so as to retain as much air as possible in the mixture.

• Allow melted butter to cool for a few minutes before mixing with eggs.

• Use medium eggs unless otherwise stated.

• Before baking, line cake tins with nonstick baking paper or a greaseproof cake liner.

• If using a conventional oven, always bake muffins and scones towards the top of the oven. In a fan oven, the temperature is the same throughout, so this is less critical.

• If using a fan oven, lower the oven temperature by 20°C (70°F) to prevent burning before the dish is cooked through.

making chocolate decorations

The following decorations can all be stored in an airtight container in the refrigerator for a week or so before needed.

grated chocolate

Before grating, make sure the chocolate is at room temperature. Rub it over the largest grating holes directly on to some greaseproof paper. Lift up the pieces with a palette knife to use as a decoration.

chocolate curls

For a speedy decoration, use a vegetable peeler to pare off thick curls from the smooth side of a bar of chocolate. For larger, more impressive curls, pour melted chocolate into a small clean plastic tub, such as a low-fat spread container. Chill the chocolate until it is just firm, pop it out of the container and drag a peeler or cheese slicer along the base or sides.

chocolate caraque

These professional-looking curls take a little more effort, but are well worth making for a special cake or dessert. They will keep well in the refrigerator for several weeks or in the freezer for longer. Spread melted chocolate in a thin layer on a marble slab, glass chopping board or the back of a tray. Leave to set. Holding a fine-bladed knife or cheese slicer at a 45-degree angle, draw it across the chocolate so that you scrape off curls.

If the chocolate is too soft and does not curl, pop it in the refrigerator for a few minutes. If it is brittle and breaks off in thin shards, leave it at room temperature for a while or put it very briefly in the microwave before trying again.

chocolate leaves

Firm but flexible leaves, such as fresh bay or rose leaves, are best for making decorations for festive desserts and chocolate logs. Wash and dry the leaves well, then brush or spoon a little chocolate on to the underside. Leave to set, then gently peel away the leaves.

chocolate scribbles

First make a paper piping bag: fold a 25 cm (10 inch) square of greaseproof paper or nonstick baking paper diagonally in half to make a triangle. Cut along the folded line. Holding the long edge towards you, curl the right-hand point of the triangle over to meet the centre point, forming a cone. Then bring the left-hand point over the cone so that the 3 points meet. Fold the paper over several times at the points to stop it unravelling.

Half-fill the bag with melted chocolate and fold down the open end to secure the bag before snipping off the tip. Test the flow and snip off a little more for a thicker flow. If the chocolate sets in the bag, pop it briefly into the microwave until softened. Draw shapes on the paper – scribbled lines, curvy swirls or filigree patterns – and leave them to set. Peel the paper away and use the scribbles to decorate chilled desserts. Don't make the patterns too delicate or they will break.

For a shortcut, use plastic disposable piping bags or just drizzle the melted chocolate from a teaspoon.

cut-out chocolate shapes

Spread melted chocolate on a tray lined with nonstick baking paper. Leave the chocolate to set, then press out the desired shapes with pastry cutters.

five-minute fix

easy peasy chocolate sauce

Serves **4**
Preparation time **2 minutes**
Cooking time **3 minutes**

175 g (6 oz) **evaporated milk**
100 g (3½ oz) **plain dark chocolate**, broken into pieces

Tip the evaporated milk into a pan, add the chocolate and heat gently for 2–3 minutes, stirring until the chocolate is melted.

Serve immediately with the dessert of your choice. This sauce goes particularly well with ice cream.

For easy minty chocolate sauce, use 100 g (3½ oz) plain dark mint chocolate instead of plain dark chocolate. Finely chop 6 fresh mint leaves and add to the mint chocolate and evaporated milk mixture. Heat gently, stirring until the chocolate is melted.

warm chocolate fromage frais

Serves **6**
Preparation time **1 minute**
Cooking time **4 minutes**

300 g (10 oz) **plain dark chocolate**
500 g (1 lb) **fat-free fromage frais**
1 teaspoon **vanilla extract**

Melt the chocolate in a bowl over a pan of simmering water (see page 10), then remove from the heat.

Add the fromage frais and vanilla extract and quickly stir together.

Divide the chocolate fromage frais among 6 little pots or glasses and serve immediately.

For warm cappuccino fromage frais, melt the plain dark chocolate with 2 tablespoons very strong espresso coffee. Divide among 6 espresso cups, finishing each with 1 teaspoon regular fromage frais and a dusting of cocoa powder.

chocolate banana croissants

Serves **4**
Preparation time **2 minutes**
Cooking time **3 minutes**

8 croissants
2 large **bananas**, sliced
250 g (8 oz) **milk chocolate**,
  broken into squares

Cut the croissants in half horizontally, using a serrated knife. Put the bases on a baking tray.

Arrange the banana slices on top of the croissant bases. Top with the chocolate squares and cover with the croissant lids.

Bake in a preheated oven, 230°C (450°F), Gas Mark 8, for 3 minutes until the croissants are warmed through and the chocolate softened.

For blueberry, apple & white chocolate croissants, omit the bananas and milk chocolate and instead quarter, core and slice 1 dessert apple, arrange on the croissant bases and top with 100 g (3½ oz) white chocolate squares. Place 1 teaspoon raspberry jam on each croissant. Cover with the croissant lids and continue as above.

drunken chocolate pancakes

Serves **4**
Preparation time **1 minute**
Cooking time **4 minutes**

Pancakes
125 g (4 oz) **plain flour**
2 tablespoons **caster sugar**
1 **egg**
300 ml (½ pint) **milk**
butter or **vegetable oil**,
   for frying
50 g (2 oz) **plain dark**
   chocolate, broken into
   squares, to fill

Sauce
100 g (3½ oz) **butter**
100 g (3½ oz) **light**
   muscovado sugar
4 tablespoons **Rubis**
   chocolate velvet ruby
   (fortified wine with
   chocolate) or other
   chocolate liqueur or **port**

Sift the flour into a bowl, then stir in the sugar. Add the egg and a little milk, and whisk to make a stiff batter. Beat in the remaining milk.

Heat a little butter or oil in an 18 cm (7 inch) pancake pan or heavy-based frying pan until it starts to smoke. Pour off the excess and pour a little batter into the pan, tilting it until the base is coated in a thin layer. (Or, if you prefer, use a small ladle to measure the batter into the pan.) Cook for 1–2 minutes until the underside begins to turn golden.

Flip the pancake with a palette knife and cook for a further 30–45 seconds on the second side. Slide the pancake out of the pan and make the remaining pancakes, greasing the pan as necessary. Set the pancakes aside while you make the sauce.

Melt the butter in a frying pan with the light muscovado sugar, then add the Rubis chocolate velvet ruby, liqueur or port.

Divide the chocolate squares among the pancakes, then fold into halves, then quarters, and slide into the pan. Warm through for a couple of minutes and serve each pancake drenched in sauce.

For children's chocolate pancakes, make 4 pancakes as above and set aside. Make an apple sauce by heating 75 g (3 oz) butter and 75 g (3 oz) light muscovado sugar in a frying pan until melted, then adding 4 tablespoons apple juice. Fill and warm the pancake as above, using 50 g (2 oz) milk chocolate instead of plain dark chocolate. Serve drenched in the apple sauce.

toffee & chocolate popcorn

Serves **4**
Preparation time **1 minute**
Cooking time **4 minutes**

50 g (2 oz) **popping corn**
250 g (8 oz) **butter**
250 g (8 oz) **light muscovado sugar**
2 tablespoons **cocoa powder**

Microwave the popping corn in a large bowl with a lid on high (900 watts) for 4 minutes. Alternatively, cook in a pan with a lid on the hob, on a medium heat, for a few minutes until popping.

Meanwhile, gently heat the butter, muscovado sugar and cocoa powder in a pan until the sugar has dissolved and the butter has melted.

Stir the warm popcorn into the mixture and serve.

For toffee, marshmallow & nut popcorn, omit the muscovado sugar and cocoa. Microwave the popping corn as above, then gently heat 150 g (5 oz) chewy toffees, 125 g (4 oz) butter, 125 g (4 oz) marshmallows and 50 g (2 oz) plain chocolate in a pan until melted. Serve as above.

chocolate brioche sandwich

Serves **1**
Preparation time **1 minute**
Cooking time **4 minutes**

2 slices **brioche**
1 tablespoon ready-made
  chocolate spread or
  homemade **Milk & White
  Chocolate Spread** (see
  page 128)
15 g (½ oz) **butter**
2 teaspoons **golden
  granulated sugar**

Spread 1 slice of brioche with chocolate spread,
then top with the other slice.

Butter the outsides of the chocolate sandwich
and sprinkle with the sugar.

Heat a griddle, frying pan or sandwich maker, and cook
the chocolate brioche for 3 minutes, turning as needed.

For peanut & chocolate brioche sandwich, spread
1 slice brioche with 1 tablespoon chocolate spread
(use ready-made spread or make the Chocolate
Hazelnut Spread on page 128) and the other slice
with 1 tablespoon peanut butter. Mash 1 banana,
spread it on top of the peanut butter, then sandwich
with the other slice.

granola with chocolate chips

Serves **1**
Preparation time **3 minutes**
Cooking time **2 minutes**

3 tablespoons **jumbo
  porridge oats**
1 tablespoon **hazelnuts**
1 tablespoon **pistachio nuts**
1 tablespoon **mixed seeds**
  (pumpkin, hemp, sunflower,
  sesame, linseed)
2 teaspoons **light olive oil**
2 teaspoons **runny honey**

To serve
150 ml (¼ pint) **vanilla yogurt**
2 tablespoons fresh
  pomegranate seeds
2 teaspoons **plain dark
  chocolate chips**

Heat a large nonstick frying pan. Toss the oats, hazelnuts, pistachio nuts and mixed seeds in the pan for a couple of minutes.

Add the olive oil and runny honey to the mixture and stir everything together.

Tip into a bowl and top with the yogurt, pomegranate seeds and chocolate chips for a delicious breakfast.

For muesli clusters with chocolate chips, mix 200 g (7 oz) muesli in a roasting pan with 4 tablespoons mixed seeds, 3 tablespoons olive oil and 3 tablespoons honey. Bake in a preheated oven, 180°C (350°F), Gas Mark 4, for 20 minutes. Cool, then stir in 3 tablespoons plain chocolate chips. Serve the muesli clusters with vanilla yogurt. Serves 4.

frothy hot toddy chocolate drink

Serves **1**
Preparation time **2 minutes**
Cooking time **3 minutes**

1 teaspoon **cornflour**
300 ml (½ pint) **semi-
  skimmed milk**
1 teaspoon **golden
  granulated sugar**
4 squares **plain dark
  chocolate**
2 tablespoons **alcohol** of your
  choice, such as brandy, rum
  or vodka
1 teaspoon **chocolate** (plain
  dark, milk or white), grated,
  to serve

Pour the cornflour into a jug and mix in 1 tablespoon milk to make a smooth paste. Add 200 ml (7 fl oz) of the milk, the sugar, the chocolate and the alcohol.

Microwave the mixture on high (900 watts) for 2 minutes or heat in a pan on the hob. Pour the hot chocolate into a tall glass mug.

Heat the remaining milk and froth vigorously. Pour over the hot chocolate. Sprinkle over some grated chocolate and serve immediately.

For festive hot chocolate, bring 750 ml (1¼ pints) full-fat milk just to the boil. Remove from the heat and add 100 g (3½ oz) chopped plain dark chocolate, 50 g (2 oz) caster sugar, 125 g (4 oz) marshmallows and a pinch of ground cinnamon. Leave to stand while you whip 125 ml (4 fl oz) double cream until it is beginning to form soft peaks. Pour the chocolate into cups or mugs, spoon the cream on top and decorate each cup with 2 marshmallows. Serve in 4 cups or 2 large mugs.

choc cinnamon eggy bread

Serves **2**
Preparation time **2 minutes**
Cooking time **3 minutes**

2 **eggs**, lightly beaten
2 thick slices **seeded brown bread**, cut in half
15 g (½ oz) **butter**
2 tablespoons **golden caster sugar**
2 teaspoons **cocoa powder**
½ teaspoon **ground cinnamon**

Place the eggs in a shallow dish. Press the bread into the egg mixture, turning to coat well.

Melt the butter in a heavy-based pan and add the eggy bread. Cook for 3 minutes, turning as needed.

Mix the sugar, cocoa powder and cinnamon on a plate and place the hot eggy bread on top, turning as needed to coat. Serve immediately.

For chocolate cinnamon bread pudding, make the cinnamon eggy bread as above and place in a greased 600 ml (1 pint) gratin dish. Melt 50 g (2 oz) plain dark chocolate in a bowl over a pan of simmering water with 150 ml (¼ pint) milk and 5 tablespoons double cream (see page 10). Stir in any egg left over from making the eggy bread, then pour the mixture over the bread in the dish. Bake for 20 minutes in a preheated oven, 180°C (350°F), Gas Mark 4, until just firm.

chilled to thrill

chocolate orange mousse

Serves **10**
Preparation time **15 minutes**,
  plus chilling
Cooking time **5 minutes**

200 g (7 oz) **plain dark
  chocolate**
3 large **egg whites**
150 g (5 oz) **golden caster
  sugar**
275 ml (9 fl oz) **double cream**
rind of **1 orange**, finely grated
50 ml (2 fl oz) **orange liqueur**
1 orange, cut into 10 wedges

Melt the chocolate in a bowl over a pan of simmering water (see page 10), then remove from the heat.

Whisk the egg whites in a clean grease-free bowl until softly peaking. Gradually whisk in the sugar, 1 tablespoon at a time, until the mixture is smooth and glossy.

Whip the cream in another bowl with the orange rind until softly peaking (take care not to overwhip or the cream will curdle). Fold in the orange liqueur.

Pour the melted chocolate into the cream mixture and mix together quickly. Beat in a spoonful of the egg white to loosen it, then carefully fold in the rest of the egg white. Mix together gently until all the egg white is incorporated.

Spoon the chocolate mousse into 10 espresso cups or small ramekins and chill for 1 hour. Serve each with an orange wedge.

For classic chocolate mousse, replace the orange liqueur with 50 ml (2 fl oz) vodka, kirsch, brandy, whisky or Southern Comfort and omit the orange rind and orange wedges. Otherwise, prepare as above. Serve the mousse with a thin biscuit such as langue de chat or cigarette russe.

chocolate filigree torte

Serves **10**
Preparation time **30 minutes**,
  plus cooling and chilling
Cooking time **20–25 minutes**

3 eggs
75 g (3 oz) **caster sugar**
50 g (2 oz) **plain flour**
25 g (1 oz) **cocoa powder**

Filling
2 teaspoons **powdered
  gelatine**
3 tablespoons **cold water**
200 g (7 oz) **plain dark
  chocolate**
500 g (1 lb) **mascarpone
  cheese**, at room
  temperature
75 g (3 oz) **caster sugar**
1 teaspoon **vanilla essence**
200 g (7 oz) **Greek yogurt**
4 tablespoons **hot water**

Whisk the eggs and sugar in a bowl over a pan of hot water until thickened. Remove from the heat and whisk for 2 minutes. Sift over the flour and cocoa powder, then fold in. Turn into the prepared tin.

Grease and line a 23 cm (9 inch) springform or loose-based cake tin. Bake in a preheated oven, 190°C (375°F), Gas Mark 5, for 15 minutes until just firm. Cool on a wire rack.

Sprinkle the gelatine over the measured water in a bowl and leave for 5 minutes. Split the sponge and put one half in the cake tin. Stand the bowl of gelatine in a pan of hot water until the gelatine has melted.

Melt 175 g (6 oz) chocolate over a pan of simmering water (see page 10). Beat the mascarpone in a bowl with the sugar, vanilla essence, yogurt and hot water. Whisking well, gradually pour the gelatine mix into the mascarpone mix. Spoon half into a separate bowl and beat in the chocolate. Turn the chocolate mix into the tin. Cover with the second sponge, then the remaining mascarpone (if this has started to set, beat in a little hot water). Level the surface and chill for several hours.

Transfer to a serving plate. Remove the greaseproof paper. Melt the remaining chocolate and drizzle it over the top. Chill until ready to serve.

For chocolate mascarpone cheesecake, process 250 g (8 oz) chocolate digestives in a blender and add 100 g (3½ oz) melted butter. Press into the base of the prepared tin, top with the melted chocolate, then with the mascarpone filling. Chill and decorate as above.

rocky road slices

Makes **12**
Preparation time **10 minutes**,
   plus chilling
Cooking time **10 minutes**

225 g (7½ oz) **butter**
3 tablespoons **golden syrup**
50 g (2 oz) **cocoa powder**
125 g (4 oz) **digestive
   biscuits**, roughly crushed
200 g (7 oz) **marshmallows**,
   each cut into 4
75 g (3 oz) **Maltesers**,
   roughly crushed
200 g (7 oz) **milk chocolate**
200 g (7 oz) **plain dark
   chocolate**
4 tablespoons **chocolate
   sprinkles**

Melt the butter with the golden syrup and cocoa powder in a bowl over a pan of simmering water. Stir in the biscuits, marshmallows and Maltesers.

Grease a 25 x 18 cm (10 x 7 inch) tin. Chill the mixture in the prepared tin for 15 minutes.

Melt the milk and plain chocolate together in a bowl over a pan of simmering water (see page 10). Remove from the heat. Pour the chocolate over the chilled mixture and scatter with chocolate sprinkles.

Chill for 20 minutes, then cut into slices or squares.

For choc & gingernut rocky road slices, melt 75 g (3 oz) plain dark chocolate with 125 g (4 oz) milk chocolate and 175 g (6 oz) butter. Once melted, stir in 2 tablespoons golden syrup, 125 g (4 oz) roughly crushed ginger biscuits, 75 g (3 oz) toasted chopped hazelnuts, 75 g (3 oz) raisins and 75 g (3 oz) chopped chocolate and nut bar. Mix together well and pour into a lined 500 g (1 lb) loaf tin. Chill as above, before slicing to serve.

flaky chocolate orange cups

Serves **6**
Preparation time **40 minutes**,
 plus chilling and freezing
Cooking time **5 minutes**

Cups
225 g (7½ oz) **plain dark
 chocolate**

Filling
200 g (7 oz) **full-fat cream
 cheese**
150 ml (¼ pint) **double cream**
150 g (5 oz) **natural yogurt**
3 tablespoons **caster sugar**
finely grated rind and juice
 of 1 **orange**
3 tablespoons **orange-
 flavoured liqueur** (optional)
4 **flaky chocolate bars**
strips of **candied orange
 peel**, to decorate

Line a baking sheet with nonstick baking paper. Cut 6 strips of nonstick baking paper, each 30 x 5 cm (12 x 2 inches). Roll up a strip and place inside a 6 cm (2½ inch) pastry cutter set on the baking sheet. Open out the strip so it lines the cutter.

Melt the chocolate over a pan of simmering water (see page 10). Spoon a little melted chocolate into the cutter and, holding the cutter in place, brush the chocolate up the side of the paper to make a chocolate cup with an irregular top edge. Carefully lift away the pastry cutter (or leave in place if you have several to use) and make 5 more cups. Chill until set.

Beat the cream cheese in a bowl to soften it. Beat in the cream, yogurt, sugar, orange rind and juice and liqueur, if using. Cut 1 flaky chocolate bar lengthways into shards and reserve the best pieces for decoration. Crumble the trimmings and the remaining 3 flaky chocolate bars into the creamed mixture.

Spoon the mixture into the chocolate cups and freeze for at least 3 hours. Carefully peel away the paper cases and transfer the cups to the refrigerator for about 1 hour before serving. Alternatively, return the cups to the freezer for a later date. Serve the cups decorated with shards of flaky chocolate bar and strips of candied orange peel.

For quick lemon cheesecake cups, use 6 ready-made chocolate cupcake cases. Make the filling as above, replacing the orange rind, juice and liqueur with 5 tablespoons lemon curd. Decorate with strips of candied lemon peel instead of the orange peel.

chocolate crème brûlée

Serves **6**
Preparation time **15 minutes**, plus chilling
Cooking time **5 minutes**

575 ml (18 fl oz) **double cream**
1 **vanilla pod**, split in half lengthways
150 g (5 oz) **plain dark chocolate**, broken into pieces
6 **egg yolks**
25 g (1 oz) **golden caster sugar**
1 tablespoon **vanilla sugar**
4 tablespoons **brandy**
6 tablespoons **clotted cream**
50 g (2 oz) **dark muscovado sugar**

Heat the double cream gently with the vanilla pod until boiling. Remove from the heat, remove the vanilla pod and add the chocolate. Stir until melted.

Whisk together the egg yolks, golden caster sugar and vanilla sugar with the brandy, until the mixture becomes thick, foamy and pale. Gradually pour on the chocolate cream and whisk in, then strain back into the cleaned pan. Gently heat the mixture, stirring continuously until it has become thick and smooth.

Fill 6 heatproof glass espresso cups with the chocolate custard, then chill for at least 2 hours. Spoon a dollop of clotted cream on to each cup. Sprinkle the top of each cup with dark muscovado sugar, then use a chef's blowtorch or hot grill to caramelize the sugar.

For chocolate berry brûlée, defrost a 500 g (1 lb) packet frozen forest fruits and divide the fruits among 6 glass ramekins or heatproof espresso cups. Sprinkle 1 tablespoon golden caster sugar over each ramekin, then pour over 2 tablespoons crème de cassis per portion. Chill and finish as above.

44

wicked chocolate slices

Makes **12**
Preparation time **15 minutes**,
  plus chilling
Cooking time **3 minutes**

225 g (7½ oz) **butter**
3 tablespoons **runny honey**
3 tablespoons **cocoa powder**
300 g (10 oz) **shortcake
  biscuits**, roughly crushed
100 g (3½ oz) **white
  chocolate**
12 **white chocolate buttons**

Heat the butter, runny honey and cocoa powder in a pan until melted. Add the crushed biscuits to the chocolate mixture and stir together until all the biscuits are coated with chocolate.

Pour into a greased 18 cm (7 inch) round tin. Chill for at least 30 minutes.

Melt the white chocolate in a bowl over a pan of simmering water (see page 10). Pour over the chocolate biscuit base to cover it. Arrange the white chocolate buttons on top.

Chill for at least 30 minutes, then cut into 12 wedges.

For cookies & cream chocolate slices, replace the shortcake biscuits with 200 g (7 oz) custard cream biscuits and 100 g (3½ oz) chocolate chip cookies, all roughly crushed. Continue as above.

chocolate blueberry trifle

Serves **8**
Preparation time **30 minutes**,
  plus cooling and chilling
Cooking time **15 minutes**

150 g (5 oz) **chocolate
  cantuccini biscuits**, broken
  into pieces
100 ml (3½ fl oz) **sweet
  sherry**
275 g (9 oz) **blueberry
  no-added-sugar jam**
600 ml (1 pint) **full-fat milk**
1 **vanilla pod**
6 large **egg yolks**
2 tablespoons **golden caster
  sugar**
3 tablespoons **cornflour**

Topping
275 ml (9 fl oz) **double cream**
250 g (8 oz) **crème fraîche**
1 teaspoon **vanilla extract**
1 tablespoon **golden caster
  sugar**

To decorate
8 **chocolate cantuccini
  biscuits**, crumbled
1 tablespoon **dragees**

Place the crumbled chocolate cantuccini biscuits in a serving bowl, reserving a few pieces for decoration Drizzle over the sherry, then spread over the jam.

Pour the milk into a pan. Cut a slit down the length of the vanilla pod and scrape the seeds into the pan with the pod. Bring to the boil. Turn off the heat and leave to cool for 5 minutes.

Whisk the egg yolks, sugar and cornflour together in a bowl. Remove the vanilla pod, then whisk the warm milk into the egg mixture. Pour the custard back into the pan. Heat gently, whisking continuously, for 2–3 minutes or until the mixture thickens. Pour the custard over the jam layer. Cool and chill until firm.

Whip the cream until softly peaking, fold together with the crème fraîche, vanilla extract and sugar. Spread over the top of the custard, then dollop on a few extra spoonfuls to decorate. Sprinkle with the reserved crumbled cantuccini biscuits and the dragees.

For chocolate & forest fruits trifle, defrost a 500 g (1 lb) packet frozen forest fruits and warm the contents for a couple of minutes in a pan with 4 tablespoons crème de cassis, 2 tablespoons water and 50 g (2 oz) sugar. Lift out the fruit with a slotted spoon and place on the cantuccini biscuits, sherry and jam in the serving bowl. Mix 1 tablespoon arrowroot with 2 tablespoons cold water and add to the red fruity liquid in the pan. Heat, stirring until the sauce is thickened, then pour it over the fruits. Then prepare the vanilla custard, continuing as above.

no-bake irish coffee gateau

Serves **8**
Preparation time **30 minutes**,
  plus cooling and chilling
Cooking time **10 minutes**

2 tablespoons **instant coffee
  granules**
100 ml (3½ fl oz) **hot water**
50 g (2 oz) **caster sugar**
3 tablespoons **Irish whiskey**
300 g (10 oz) **plain dark
  chocolate**, broken into
  pieces
300 ml (½ pint) **double cream**
200 g (7 oz) **Greek yogurt**
200 g (7 oz) **savoiardi
  biscuits** or **sponge fingers**

To decorate
**plain dark or milk chocolate
  curls** (see page 12)
cocoa powder, for dusting

Dissolve the coffee granules in a pan in the hot water.
Add the sugar and heat gently until the sugar dissolves.
Bring to the boil and boil rapidly for 1 minute. Remove
from the heat and leave to cool. Stir in the whiskey.

Melt the chocolate with half the cream in a bowl over
a pan of simmering water (see page 10). Remove from
the heat and stir in the yogurt and remaining cream.
Leave to thicken slightly.

Spread a thin layer of the chocolate mixture on to a
flat plate, to make a 23 x 10 cm (9 x 4 inch) rectangle.
Dip one-third of the biscuits or sponge fingers in the
coffee syrup so they are softened but not soggy.

Arrange the dipped biscuits or fingers side by side
on the chocolate, then spread over more chocolate
mixture. Dip half the remaining biscuits or fingers in the
syrup and arrange them as before over the chocolate.
Spread more chocolate mixture on top, then cover with
the remaining syrup-dipped biscuits or fingers.

Spread the remaining chocolate mixture over the top
and sides of the cake to cover it completely, smoothing
with the knife. Chill for 3–4 hours until set. Decorate
with chocolate curls and dust with cocoa powder.

For no-bake cappuccino gateau, replace the Irish
whiskey with 3 tablespoons Kahula and use 300 g
(10 oz) white chocolate instead of the plain dark
chocolate. Create a chocolate rectangle as above,
cover with the soaked sponge fingers, then sprinkle
with 25 g (2 oz) grated milk chocolate and continue
layering. Chill and finish as above.

silky chocolate tarts

Serves **8**
Preparation time **10 minutes**,
  plus chilling
Cooking time **5 minutes**

225 g (7½ oz) **plain dark
  chocolate**
300 ml (½ pint) **double cream**
8 ready-made **all-butter
  pastry cases**, about 7 cm
  (3 inches) in diameter
2 tablespoons **cocoa powder**
  (optional)
200 g (7 oz) fresh
  raspberries
plain dark chocolate curls
  (see page 12)

Melt the chocolate in a bowl over a pan of simmering water (see page 10). Warm the cream gently in a pan, then stir into the warm chocolate.

Arrange the pastry cases on a tray. Pour in the chocolate cream and chill for 1 hour.

Top the tarts with raspberries, dust with cocoa powder, if using, and finish each tart with a couple of long chocolate curls.

For chocolate & strawberry tarts, use 225 g (7½ oz) milk chocolate instead of the plain dark chocolate and top the tarts with 200 g (7 oz) fresh sliced strawberries instead of the raspberries. Dust with 1 tablespoon golden caster sugar instead of the cocoa powder.

tiramisu cheesecake

Serves **8–10**
Preparation time **20–25 minutes**, plus cooling and chilling
Cooking time **50 minutes**

20 **sponge fingers**
175 g (6 oz) **plain dark chocolate**
750 g (1½ lb) **mascarpone cheese**
150 g (5 oz) **golden caster sugar**
3 **eggs**, separated
40 g (1½ oz) **plain white flour**
3 tablespoons **grappa**
1 teaspoon **vanilla extract**
2 tablespoons very strong **espresso coffee**
2 tablespoons **coffee liqueur**

To decorate
plain dark and marbled white and milk chocolate curls (see page 12)
2 tablespoons **golden icing sugar**, sifted

Line a 23 cm (9 inch) springform tin with a greaseproof cake liner or nonstick baking paper. Arrange the sponge fingers over the base, cutting them to fit as needed.

Melt the chocolate in a bowl over a pan of simmering water (see page 10).

Blend the mascarpone, sugar and egg yolks in a food processor until smooth. Remove one-third of the mix to another bowl, add the flour, grappa and vanilla extract and mix well. Add the melted chocolate, espresso coffee and coffee liqueur to the mascarpone in the processor and blend to combine. Turn into a large bowl.

Whisk the egg whites in a grease-free bowl until they are softly peaking. Fold two-thirds into the chocolate mixture and one-third into the white mixture. Pour the chocolate mixture into the sponge finger-lined tin. Pour on the chocolate mascarpone mixture, then spoon on the white mixture to cover the chocolate layer.

Bake in a preheated oven, 200°C (400°F), Gas Mark 6, for 45 minutes, then turn off the oven, leave the oven door slightly ajar and leave to cool in the oven.

Chill for 3 hours when cooled. Arrange the chocolate curls on top, dust with icing sugar and serve.

For easy vanilla, chocolate & banana cheesecake, use a large sponge flan case in place of the fingers. Mix the mascarpone, sugar and yolks, then add the flour, 100 ml (4 fl oz) milk, 1 tablespoon vanilla extract, the melted chocolate and 2 mashed ripe bananas. Omit the grappa, coffee and liqueur. Bake as above, then decorate with 75 g (3 oz) banana chips.

white chocolate & berry trifle

Serves **8**
Preparation time **40 minutes**,
  plus chilling
Cooking time **15 minutes**

1 kg (2 lb) **frozen summer
  berries**
100 g (3½ oz) **golden caster
  sugar**
2 teaspoons **arrowroot**
225 g (7½ oz) **ratafia
  biscuits**, plus 8 more,
  crumbled, to decorate
5 tablespoons **red vermouth**
275 ml (9 fl oz) **double cream**
200 g (7 oz) **white chocolate
  with vanilla**
500 g (1 lb) ready-made
  custard, at room
  temperature
500 ml (17 fl oz) **Greek
  strained yogurt**
2 tablespoons **light
  muscovado sugar**

Heat the berries gently in a pan with the golden caster sugar for about 5 minutes, just until the sugar has dissolved and the fruits have thawed.

Drain the berries through a sieve and return the juice to the pan and warm it through. Mix the arrowroot with 1 tablespoon cold water to make a smooth paste. Add to the warm juices in the pan and stir together until thickened and smooth.

Arrange the ratafias in the base of a large glass compôte or individual compôtes. Pour over the red vermouth. Spoon over the fruits and thickened juice.

Whip the cream lightly and reserve half in the fridge. Melt the white chocolate in a bowl over a pan of simmering water (see page 10). Stir in half the custard and mix well. Remove from the heat, add the rest of the custard and fold in the whipped cream. Spoon on top of the fruits. Chill for 1 hour.

Mix together the yogurt, light muscovado sugar and chilled whipped cream from the fridge. Spoon over the top of the custard, smooth over the surface and sprinkle with the extra crumbled ratafia biscuits.

For tropical fruits trifle, replace the frozen summer berries with 2 x 500 g (1 lb) bags frozen tropical fruits and cook as above. Replace the red vermouth with 5 tablespoons sweet white wine and drizzle over the ratafias. Top with the white chocolate custard and finish with cream as above.

coffee chocolate bavarois

Serves **10**
Preparation time **45 minutes**,
  plus freezing and chilling
Cooking time **10 minutes**

1 litre (1¾ pints) **single cream**
150 g (5 oz) **plain dark
  chocolate**, chopped
2 teaspoons **cornflour**
150 g (5 oz) **golden caster
  sugar**
8 **egg yolks**
25 g (1 oz) **powdered
  gelatine**
1 tablespoon fresh **espresso
  coffee**, extremely strong
4 tablespoons **coffee liqueur**

Line a 1 kg (2 lb) loaf tin with baking paper and place in the freezer to chill.

Heat half the cream gently in a pan. Add the chocolate and stir until melted. Remove from the heat.

Put half the cornflour, half the sugar and 4 egg yolks in a bowl. Put the remaining cornflour, sugar and yolks in a second bowl. Stir, then slowly whisk the chocolate cream into one bowl. Return to the pan and heat gently, stirring until slightly thickened and smooth. Whisk in half the powdered gelatine, then pour into a jug.

Pour half the chocolate cream into the base of the prepared loaf tin. Freeze uncovered, on a flat surface, for 45 minutes until just set.

Combine the remaining cream, espresso coffee and coffee liqueur in a pan over a low heat. Whisk this into the mixture in the second bowl, transfer to the pan and warm through. Add the rest of the gelatine and whisk together. Remove from the heat and pour into a jug.

Pour half the coffee cream over the set chocolate cream and refreeze for another 30 minutes or until just set. Pour over the remaining chocolate cream and freeze for 20 minutes, until just set, then pour on the final coffee cream layer. Chill for 4 hours. Run a knife around the sides, turn on to a board and slice to serve.

For chocolate orange & amaretti bavarois, sprinkle 75 g (3 oz) crushed amaretti over the base of the tin before freezing. Replace the coffee with 1 tablespoon orange juice and 2 tablespoons finely grated orange rind. Use orange liqueur in place of the coffee liqueur.

triple chocolate brûlée

Serves **6**
Preparation time **30 minutes**,
  plus freezing and chilling
Cooking time **5 minutes**

8 egg yolks
150 g (5 oz) **golden caster
  sugar**
600 ml (1 pint) **double cream**
125 g (4 oz) **plain dark
  chocolate**, finely chopped
125 g (4 oz) **white chocolate**,
  finely chopped
125 g (4 oz) **milk chocolate**,
  finely chopped
3 tablespoons **Amaretto di
  Saronno** or **brandy**
  (optional)

To decorate
golden caster sugar, to
  sprinkle
plain dark, milk and
  white chocolate curls
  (see page 12, optional)

Mix the egg yolks and half the sugar in a bowl, using a fork. Pour the cream into a pan and bring almost to a boil. Gradually beat the cream into the yolk mixture to make a custard.

Strain the custard into a jug, then divide equally among 3 bowls. Stir a different chocolate into each bowl, adding 1 tablespoon liqueur, if using. Stir until melted.

Divide the plain dark chocolate custard between 6 ramekins. When cool, transfer the dishes to the freezer for 10 minutes to set.

Remove the dishes from the freezer. Stir the white chocolate custard and spoon it over the dark layer in the dishes. Return to the freezer for 10 minutes.

Remove the dishes from the freezer. Stir the milk chocolate custard and spoon into the dishes. Chill in the refrigerator for 3–4 hours until set. About 25 minutes before serving, sprinkle with the remaining sugar and caramelize with a blow torch or under a hot grill. Leave at room temperature until ready to eat, then decorate with chocolate curls, if desired.

For speedy triple chocolate brûlée, omit the egg yolks, cream and Amaretto or brandy. Mix 600 ml (1 pint) strained Greek yogurt, 200 ml (7 fl oz) crème fraîche and 1 teaspoon vanilla extract, then stir in the golden caster sugar. Divide among 3 bowls and stir a different type of chopped chocolate into each bowl. Spoon the 3 mixtures into the ramekins in 3 layers (no need to freeze in between), then chill in the refrigerator for 30 minutes before serving.

chocolate cheesecake

Serves **14**
Preparation time **45 minutes**,
  plus cooling and chilling
Cooking time **50 minutes**

225 g (7½ oz) **digestive
  biscuits**, broken into crumbs
65 g (2½ oz) **butter**, melted
225 g (7½ oz) **plain dark
  chocolate**
225 g (7½ oz) **white
  chocolate**
350 g (11½ oz) **cream
  cheese**
500 g (1 lb) **fromage frais**
175 g (6 oz) **golden caster
  sugar**
3 **eggs**

Grease and line the base of a 23 cm (9 inch) springform tin. Mix the biscuit crumbs with the melted butter and press into the base of the prepared tin.

Melt the plain dark and white chocolate in separate bowls over pans of simmering water (see page 10).

Whiz the cream cheese, fromage frais, sugar and eggs in a food processor until smooth. Tip half the mix into the melted plain dark chocolate, and the other half into the melted white chocolate, and stir until smooth. Spoon half the white chocolate mix over the biscuit base, top with the dark chocolate mix, then finish with the rest of the white chocolate mix. Drag a skewer through the white and dark layers to marble the top.

Bake in a preheated oven, 160°C (325°F), Gas Mark 3, for 50 minutes until slightly risen and just firm to the touch. Leave to cool, then chill.

For choc & raspberry cheesecake, use chocolate digestive biscuits and replace the 2 types of chocolate with 450 g (14½ oz) plain dark chocolate. Melt the chocolate with 50 g (2 oz) butter, then stir in 2 tablespoons cocoa powder. Combine 500 g (1 lb) cream cheese, 200 g (7 oz) golden caster sugar and 3 large eggs and mix with the melted chocolate. Stir in 600 ml (1 pint) sour cream. Bake, cool and chill as above. Decorate with 250 g (8 oz) raspberries.

boozy chocolate panna cotta

Serves **2**
Preparation time **10 minutes**,
  plus chilling
Cooking time **5 minutes**

125 ml (4 fl oz) **double cream**
150 ml (¼ pint) **milk**
3 tablespoons **light
  muscovado sugar**
50 ml (2 fl oz) **chocolate
  liqueur**
40 g (1½ oz) **plain dark
  chocolate**, roughly chopped
1½ teaspoons **powdered
  gelatine**
1 teaspoon **vanilla extract**
4 **white chocolate coffee
  beans**

Heat 100 ml (3½ fl oz) cream in a small pan with the milk, sugar, 1 tablespoon chocolate liqueur and the chocolate, gently stirring until the chocolate has melted. Bring to the boil.

Remove the pan from the heat, sprinkle over the gelatine and leave for 5 minutes. Stir together, add the vanilla extract and mix. Strain the mixture into a jug.

Grease and line 2 x 150 ml (¼ pint) pudding basins with clingfilm. Pour the mixture into the prepared pudding basins and chill for 2 hours.

Turn on to plates and remove the clingfilm. Mix together the rest of the cream and chocolate liqueur and drizzle around the panna cotta. Finish with a white chocolate coffee bean on each.

For white chocolate & honey panna cotta, use 1 tablespoon golden caster sugar and 2 tablespoons honey instead of the light muscovado sugar. Substitute the plain dark chocolate for 75 g (3 oz) white chocolate. Proceed as above, serving with a drizzle of chocolate liqueur and a dark chocolate coffee bean on each.

pyramid slices

Serves **10**
Preparation time **20 minutes**,
  plus cooling and setting
Cooking time **10 minutes**

300 g (10 oz) **milk chocolate**,
  broken into pieces
100 ml (3½ fl oz) **evaporated
  milk**
175 g (6 oz) **digestive
  biscuits**, broken into small
  pieces
125 g (4 oz) stoned **dates,
  prunes** or **dried apricots**,
  roughly chopped
100 g (3½ oz) **mixed nuts**,
  chopped
50 g (2 oz) **plain dark
  chocolate**

Heat the milk chocolate gently in a heavy-based pan
with the evaporated milk, stirring frequently, until the
chocolate has melted. Remove from the heat and
transfer to a bowl. Leave until cool, but not set. Stir
in the biscuits, dried fruit and nuts.

Grease the base and 3 sides of a deep 18 cm (7 inch)
square cake tin and line with clingfilm. Prop up one
side of the tin so that it sits at an angle of 45 degrees
and the unlined side of the tin is uppermost. Spoon in
the cake mixture and level the surface. Leave until firm,
then transfer to the refrigerator to set completely.
Remove the cake from the tin and peel away the film.

Melt the plain dark chocolate (see page 10). Using a
teaspoon, drizzle lines of melted chocolate over the
cake. Leave to set again, then serve thinly sliced.

For refrigerator bars, replace the digestive biscuits
with 175 g (6 oz) shortbread biscuits, broken into
pieces, and use 125 g (4 oz) mixed dried red berries
and 100 g (3½ oz) crushed ratafia biscuits instead of
the mixed fruit and nuts. Line a 1 kg (2 lb) loaf tin with
clingfilm and follow the recipe described above. To
decorate, melt 50 g (2 oz) white chocolate and drizzle
over the top and sides of the cake.

double chocolate ice cream pie

Serves **8**
Preparation time **15 minutes**,
  plus freezing
Cooking time **5 minutes**

500 ml (17 fl oz) good-quality
  chocolate ice cream
75 g (3 oz) **olive oil spread**
200 g (7 oz) **plain dark
  chocolate digestive
  biscuits,** broken into coarse
  crumbs
2 large **bananas,** sliced
1 tablespoon **lemon juice**
1 king-size **caramel chocolate
  bar,** cut into thin slices

Remove the ice cream from the freezer and let it
soften. Grease and line the base of a 20 cm (8 inch)
loose-based fluted flan tin.

Melt the olive oil spread in a pan. Combine the melted
olive oil spread with the biscuit crumbs and press the
mixture into the base of the prepared tin.

Toss the bananas in the lemon juice and scatter over
the biscuit base.

Spread the ice cream on top of the bananas, using a
palette knife to evenly cover them.

Scatter the chocolate bar slices over the top of the ice
cream. Freeze for at least 1 hour before serving.

For banoffee ice cream pie, use 200 g (7 oz) plain
digestive biscuits instead of the chocolate biscuits
and top with 400 g (13 oz) dulce de leche (toffee
caramel). Add the bananas in lemon juice and finish
as above, using 500 ml (17 fl oz) good-quality caramel
ice cream instead of the chocolate ice cream.

hot
puddings

gooey mocha fondant puddings

Makes **10**
Preparation time **15 minutes**
Cooking time **20 minutes**

200 g (7 oz) **plain dark chocolate**
250 g (8 oz) **butter**
4 tablespoons **coffee liqueur**
1 tablespoon extremely strong **espresso coffee**
4 large **eggs**
2 large **egg yolks**
125 g (4 oz) **golden caster sugar**
65 g (2½ oz) **wholemeal plain flour**, sifted
2 tablespoons **golden icing sugar**, to dust

Melt the chocolate with the butter in a bowl over a pan of simmering water (see page 10). Remove from the heat once melted and add the coffee liqueur and espresso coffee, stirring until glossy.

Whisk the eggs, egg yolks and sugar in a bowl for about 10 minutes until pale, thick, foamy and doubled in volume. Pour the chocolate mixture into the whisked egg mixture and add the flour and any bran left in the sieve. Fold everything together gently.

Grease 10 ovenproof 150 ml (¼ pint) cups or ramekins. Ladle the mixture into the prepared cups or ramekins and place on a baking sheet. (They can be chilled for several hours before baking.) Bake in a preheated oven, 200°C (400°F), Gas Mark 6, for 10−12 minutes until they are just firm around the edges and squidgy in the centre.

Dust with icing sugar and serve immediately (the longer you leave them before eating the firmer the centres will become).

For chocolate orange fondant puddings, use 200 g (7 oz) orange-flavoured chocolate instead of the plain dark chocolate and 4 tablespoons orange liqueur instead of the coffee liqueur. Replace the espresso coffee with 4 tablespoons orange juice and 2 tablespoons finely grated orange rind. Prepare following the method described above.

chocolate croissant pudding

Serves **3**
Preparation time **15 minutes**
Cooking time **15 minutes**

2 tablespoons **cocoa powder**
3 tablespoons **icing sugar**
100 ml (3½ fl oz) **milk**
500 g (1 lb) ready-made **custard**
3 large **croissants**
6 tablespoons ready-made **chocolate spread** or homemade **Chocolate Hazelnut Spread** (see page 128)

Mix the cocoa powder and 2 tablespoons icing sugar in a jug and gradually add the milk to form a smooth paste. Slowly stir in the custard and whisk together until smooth.

Cut the croissants in half horizontally and spread each cut side with the chocolate spread. Sandwich together again and arrange in a shallow ovenproof dish.

Drizzle the chocolate custard around the croissants and bake in a preheated oven, 200°C (400°F), Gas Mark 6, for 15 minutes. Dust with the remaining sifted icing sugar to serve.

For chocolate panettone pudding, make up the chocolate custard as above, adding 2 tablespoons brandy and the finely grated rind of 1 lemon. Spread 25 g (1 oz) butter on 6 slices panettone. Arrange the panettone in an ovenproof dish, pour over the chocolate custard and bake as above, dusting with icing sugar to serve.

chocolate risotto

Serves **4**
Preparation time **5 minutes**
Cooking time **20 minutes**

600 ml (1 pint) **milk**
25 g (1 oz) **golden caster sugar**
50 g (2 oz) **butter**
125 g (4 oz) **arborio or carnaroli rice**
50 g (2 oz) **hazelnuts**, toasted and chopped
50 g (2 oz) **sultanas**
125 g (4 oz) good-quality **plain dark chocolate**, grated, plus some to decorate
brandy (optional)

Heat the milk and golden caster sugar in a pan to simmering point.

Melt the butter in a heavy-based pan, add the rice and stir well to coat the grains. Add a ladleful of the hot milk to the rice and stir well. When the rice has absorbed the milk, add another ladleful. Continue to add milk in stages and stir until it is all absorbed. The rice should be slightly *al dente*, with a creamy sauce.

Add the hazelnuts, sultanas and chocolate and mix quickly. Serve decorated with a little grated chocolate. Don't overmix the chocolate as a marbled effect looks good. For a special treat, add a splash of brandy just before decorating and serving the risotto.

For chocolate & orange rice pudding, add the finely grated rind of 1 orange when heating the milk and sugar. Make the risotto as above, then stir in 2 tablespoons orange juice, 125 g (4 oz) grated milk chocolate and 75 g (3 oz) chopped tropical dried fruit instead of the hazelnuts, sultanas and plain dark chocolate. Reserve a little of the grated chocolate for decoration.

squidgy cakes & cherry compôte

Makes **6**
Preparation time **20 minutes**,
 plus cooling
Cooking time **18 minutes**

Compôte
50 g (2 oz) **golden caster
 sugar**
2 tablespoons **water**
125 g (4 oz) fresh **cherries**,
 halved and pitted
150 ml (¼ pint) **Moscato wine**
100 g (3½ oz) fresh **cherries**,
 whole with stems

Cakes
175 g (6 oz) **plain dark
 chocolate**
175 g (6 oz) **butter**
4 **eggs**
4 **egg yolks**
75 g (3 oz) **golden caster
 sugar**
75 g (3 oz) **plain flour**, sifted

Heat the golden caster sugar in a pan with the water for about 2 minutes until the sugar has dissolved and starts to turn syrupy. Add the halved cherries and cook, stirring, for 1 minute. Pour in the Moscato wine and bring to the boil, bubble to reduce for 5 minutes, then add the whole cherries and cook for 1 minute. Cool.

Melt the chocolate with the butter in a bowl over a pan of simmering water (see page 10).

Whisk the whole eggs, egg yolks and golden caster sugar until very pale, foamy and doubled in volume. Pour in the melted chocolate mixture and gently fold in, then fold in the flour.

Grease 6 cooking rings, 6 x 8 cm (2½ x 3½ inches), and arrange them on a baking tray lined with nonstick baking paper, or use base-lined tart tins or Yorkshire pudding tins. Turn the mixture into the rings or tins and bake in a preheated oven, 190°C (375°F), Gas Mark 5, for 8 minutes until firm on the outside and squidgy in the centre. (Unbaked cakes can be chilled for up to 5 hours before baking for 9 minutes.)

Remove the rings or remove from the tins. Drizzle with the syrup and serve with the cherry compôte, arranging 2 whole cherries with stems on each plate.

For white chocolate cakes with apricot compôte, quarter and pitt 225 g (7½ oz) fresh apricots. Use 125 g (4 oz) apricot quarters instead of the halved cherries and 100 g (3½ oz) apricot quarters instead of the whole cherries. Add a cinnamon stick to the pan when poaching the apricots. For the cakes, use 175 g (6 oz) white chocolate instead of the dark chocolate.

wicked chocolate pudding

Serves **6**
Preparation time **20 minutes**
Cooking time **about 2 hours**

75 g (3 oz) **butter**
150 g (5 oz) **light muscovado sugar**
finely grated rind of 1 **orange**
2 **eggs**
150 g (5 oz) **self-raising flour**
25 g (1 oz) **cocoa powder**
½ teaspoon **bicarbonate of soda**
100 g (3½ oz) **milk chocolate**, chopped
pouring cream or ready-made **custard**, to serve

Sauce
125 g (4 oz) **light muscovado sugar**
75 g (3 oz) **butter**
4 tablespoons **orange juice**
50 g (2 oz) **dates**, stoned and chopped

Put the butter, sugar, orange rind and eggs in a large bowl, then sift in the flour, cocoa powder and bicarbonate of soda and beat well until creamy. Stir in the chocolate.

Grease the inside of a 1.2 litre (2 pint) pudding basin and line the base with nonstick baking paper. Turn the mixture into the basin and level the surface. Cover with a double thickness of nonstick baking paper and a sheet of foil, securing them under the rim of the basin with string.

Bring a 5 cm (2 inch) depth of water to the boil in a large pan. Lower in the pudding basin and cover the pan with a lid. Steam for 1¾ hours, topping up the water occasionally, if necessary.

Heat the sugar, butter and orange juice gently in a small pan until the sugar dissolves. Bring to the boil and boil for 1 minute. Stir in the dates and cook for 1 minute. To serve, invert the pudding on to a serving plate and pour the sauce over the top. Serve with pouring cream or custard on the side.

For chocolate custard, to serve instead of the orange and date sauce and pouring cream or custard, gently melt 50 g (2 oz) chopped plain dark chocolate with 600 ml (1 pint) single cream in a bowl over a pan of simmering water (see page 10). Remove from the heat. Mix together 4 egg yolks, 50 g (2 oz) golden caster sugar and 1 tablespoon cornflour. Add the warm chocolate cream, whisk, return to the pan and stir until thickened.

chocolate brioche pudding

Serves **4**
Preparation time **10 minutes**,
  plus cooling
Cooking time **30 minutes**

15 g (½ oz) **butter**
75 g (3 oz) **plain dark
  chocolate**, broken into
  pieces
1 tablespoon **caster sugar**
300 ml (½ pint) **semi-
  skimmed milk**
2 large **eggs**
3 **brioche rolls**, each cut into
  4 slices
icing sugar, for dusting
reduced-fat crème fraîche,
  to serve (optional)

Place the butter, chocolate, sugar and milk in a small pan and heat gently until the sugar has dissolved and the chocolate has melted. Set aside to cool a little.

Whisk the eggs in a medium bowl, then gradually add the chocolate mixture, whisking continuously.

Grease a shallow 18 x 23 cm (7 x 9 inch) ovenproof dish. Soak each slice of brioche in the chocolate mixture, then layer the slices in the dish.

Pour over any excess liquid, then bake in a preheated oven, 200°C (400°F), Gas Mark 6, for 25–30 minutes until risen and just set. Dust with icing sugar and serve with some reduced-fat crème fraîche on the side.

For butterscotch brioche pudding, mix 100 g (3½ oz) butter and 100 g (3½ oz) demerara sugar in a pan. Add 50 g (2 oz) drinking chocolate and heat gently, stirring until dissolved. Gradually add 300 ml (½ pint) milk and continue stirring until smooth. In a medium bowl whisk 2 large eggs, then slowly add the butterscotch chocolate custard, whisking continuously. Return to the pan and heat gently, stirring until slightly thickened and smooth. Assemble the pudding and bake as above.

pancakes with chocolate & ricotta

Makes **4**

Preparation time **25–30 minutes**

Cooking time **25–35 minutes**

Pancakes
125 g (4 oz) **plain flour**
2 tablespoons **golden caster sugar**
1 **egg**
300 ml (½ pint) **milk**
butter or **vegetable oil**, for frying

Filling
1 piece **stem ginger**, about 15 g (½ oz), finely chopped
2 tablespoons **caster sugar**, plus extra for dusting
250 g (8 oz) **ricotta cheese**
50 g (2 oz) **raisins**
150 g (5 oz) **white chocolate**, finely chopped
3 tablespoons **double cream**

Sauce
125 g (4 oz) **caster sugar**
100 ml (3½ fl oz) **water**
200 g (7 oz) **plain dark chocolate**, broken in pieces
25 g (1 oz) **butter**

Sift the flour into a bowl, then stir in the sugar. Add the egg and a little milk, and whisk to make a stiff batter. Beat in the remaining milk.

Heat a little butter or oil in an 18 cm (7 inch) pan until it starts to smoke. Pour off the excess and pour in a little batter, tilting until the base is thinly coated. Cook for 1–2 minutes until the underside begins to turn golden.

Flip the pancake with a palette knife and cook for a further 30–45 seconds on the second side. Slide out of the pan and make the remaining pancakes.

Mix the ginger in a bowl with the sugar, ricotta, raisins, white chocolate and cream. Place spoonfuls of the filling in the centres of the pancakes and fold them into quarters, enclosing the filling.

Place the pancakes in a lightly greased ovenproof dish and dust with sugar. Heat in a preheated oven, 200°C (400°F), Gas Mark 6, for 10 minutes.

Dissolve the caster sugar in the water, then boil rapidly for 1 minute. Remove from the heat and add the chocolate. Leave until melted, then stir in the butter for a smooth glossy sauce to serve with the hot filled pancakes.

For orange, apricot & cream cheese filling, mix together the finely grated rind of 1 orange with 1 tablespoon orange juice, 2 tablespoons golden caster sugar, 250 g (8 oz) reduced-fat cream cheese, 50 g (2 oz) chopped dried apricots and 150 g (5 oz) chopped white chocolate. Stir together, adding 3 tablespoons double cream if necessary to soften.

white chocolate soufflés

Makes **4**

Preparation time **30 minutes**, plus cooling

Cooking time **15–20 minutes**

butter, for greasing

75 g (3 oz) **caster sugar**, plus 4 teaspoons for lining the dishes

3 **egg yolks**

40 g (1½ oz) **plain flour**

250 ml (8 fl oz) **milk**

175 g (6 oz) **white chocolate**, roughly chopped

1 teaspoon **vanilla essence**

5 **egg whites**

drinking chocolate powder and **icing sugar**, sifted, for dusting

Sauce

150 g (5 oz) **plain dark chocolate**, broken into pieces

125 ml (4 fl oz) **milk**

4 tablespoons **double cream**

25 g (1 oz) **caster sugar**

Butter lightly 4 small soufflé dishes, 10 cm (4 inches) in diameter and 6 cm (2½ inches) deep, then swirl 1 teaspoon caster sugar around each dish and shake off any excess. Stand the dishes on a baking tray.

Beat half the remaining caster sugar and the egg yolks in a bowl until thick and mousse-like. Sift the flour over the surface, then gently fold it in.

Bring the milk just to the boil in a pan, then gradually whisk it into the egg yolk mixture. Return the milk to the pan and cook over a medium heat, stirring until thickened and smooth. Remove the pan from the heat, add half the white chocolate and stir until melted. Mix in the vanilla essence, cover and leave to cool.

Whisk the egg whites into stiff peaks. Gradually whisk in the remaining caster sugar until thick and glossy. Fold a large spoonful of egg whites into the cooled milk mixture to loosen it, then fold in the remaining white chocolate. Gently fold in the remaining egg whites.

Spoon into the soufflé dishes and bake in a preheated oven, 220°C (425°F), Gas Mark 7, for 10–12 minutes until the soufflés are well risen.

Heat all the sauce ingredients gently in a pan, stirring until smooth, then pour into a serving jug. Dust the tops of the soufflés with chocolate powder and icing sugar and serve immediately drizzled with the sauce.

For berry compôte, to serve instead of the chocolate sauce, heat 500 g (1 lb) frozen mixed berries with 50 g (2 oz) caster sugar and 6 tablespoons cassis until the fruit is just softened.

celebration time

white chocolate torte

Serves **8**
Preparation time **10 minutes**,
  plus cooling
Cooking time **45 minutes**

475 g (15 oz) **white chocolate**
125 g (4 oz) **butter**
3 large **eggs**, separated
125 g (4 oz) **golden caster sugar**
75 g (3 oz) **wholemeal self-raising flour**, sifted
50 g (2 oz) **ground almonds**

Melt 225 g (7½ oz) chocolate with the butter in a bowl over a pan of simmering water (see page 10). Reserve the rest of the chocolate for decoration.

Beat the egg yolks and sugar until pale, thick and foamy. Slowly whisk in the melted chocolate. Fold in the flour (and any bran in the sieve) and ground almonds.

Whisk the egg whites in a large grease-free bowl until softly peaking. Beat a large spoonful of the egg whites into the chocolate mixture, to loosen it slightly, then fold in the remainder using a large metal spoon.

Grease a 20 cm (8 inch) springform tin and line with a greaseproof cake liner or nonstick baking paper. Pour the mixture into the tin and bake in a preheated oven, 180°C (350°F), Gas Mark 4, for 45 minutes or until a skewer pushed into the centre comes out clean.

Cool in the tin for 10 minutes, then release and remove the sides of the tin and continue cooling. Grate half the reserved white chocolate (see page 12) and melt the rest in a bowl over a pan of simmering water. Spread the melted chocolate over the top of the cooled cake, then scatter over the gratings.

For milk chocolate brandy torte, replace the white chocolate with 475 g (15 oz) milk chocolate. Replace the caster sugar with 125 g (4 oz) light soft brown sugar. Beat the sugar with the yolks, then whisk in 50 ml (2 fl oz) brandy and 225 g (7½ oz) melted milk chocolate (reserving the rest for decoration). Fold in the flour and almonds, then continue as above.

marbled chocolate bombe cake

Serves **20**

Preparation time **1 hour**, plus cooling

Cooking time 1¼ **hours**

250 g (8 oz) **butter**

250 g (8 oz) **golden caster sugar**

few drops **vanilla extract**

5 **eggs**, lightly beaten

250 g (8 oz) **self-raising flour**, plus extra for dusting

100 g (3½ oz) **white chocolate chips**

100 g (3½ oz) **plain dark chocolate chips**

25 g (1 oz) **cocoa powder**

75 g (3 oz) warm **apricot jam**

1 **white chocolate coffee bean**

Syrup

50 g (2 oz) **golden caster sugar**

100 ml (3½ fl oz) **water**

50 ml (2 fl oz) **orange liqueur**

Marzipan

1 tablespoon **liquid glucose** or **orange liqueur**

450 g (14½ oz) **white marzipan**

50 g (2 oz) **cocoa powder**

Cream together the butter, sugar and vanilla extract until pale and fluffy, then gradually beat in the eggs. Fold in the flour. Spoon half the mix into another bowl. Add the white chocolate chips to 1 bowl and the plain dark chocolate chips and cocoa powder to the other. Mix each until combined.

Grease a 23 cm (9 inch) dome-shaped daisy tin or heatproof bowl, then dust with flour. Spoon in the mixtures alternately, then run a knife through the mixtures to marble them. Make a dip in the centre and bake in a preheated oven, 180°C (350°F), Gas Mark 4, for 1–1¼ hours. Cool for 15 minutes, then turn out on to a wire rack and cool for a further 30 minutes.

Boil the sugar and measured water in a pan for several minutes until the liquid becomes syrupy. Remove from the heat, then add the orange liqueur.

Knead the liquid glucose or orange liqueur and cocoa powder into the marzipan. Roll out two-thirds of the marzipan between 2 sheets of baking paper to a 40 cm (16 inch) circle, then mould large ripples across it.

Trim the cake base if needed and turn on to a serving plate. Spoon over the syrup and brush with warm apricot jam. Drape over the marzipan and trim off the excess at the base. Pat the sides to make an edge.

Roll out the remaining chocolate marzipan and cut 20 x 2.5 cm (1 inch) flower shapes. Reroll the trimmings and cut 3 larger but differently sized flower shapes and stack these on top. Arrange the small flowers at the base of the cake. Finish the topping with 1 white chocolate coffee bean.

really moist chocolate slice

Serves **12–14**
Preparation time **20 minutes**, plus cooling
Cooking time **45 minutes**

250 g (8 oz) **plain dark chocolate**
250 g (8 oz) **butter**
5 **eggs**
50 g (2 oz) **light muscovado sugar**
125 g (4 oz) **self-raising flour**
75 g (3 oz) **ground almonds**

Chocolate cream
150 ml (¼ pint) **double cream**
150 g (5 oz) **plain dark chocolate**, chopped

Melt the chocolate with the butter in a bowl over a pan of simmering water (see page 10).

Beat the eggs and sugar until slightly thickened. Sift the flour over the mixture, then add the almonds and chocolate mixture and fold in until evenly combined.

Grease and line a 23 cm (9 inch) square cake tin. Turn the mixture into the tin and bake in a preheated oven, 160°C (325°F), Gas Mark 3, for about 35 minutes until just firm. Transfer to a wire rack to cool.

Heat the cream in a pan until almost boiling. Remove the pan from the heat and add the chocolate. Leave until the chocolate has melted, then stir until smooth. Transfer to a bowl and leave to cool until thickened.

Slice off the top of the cake if it has risen in the centre. Halve the cake horizontally and sandwich the halves with one-third of the chocolate cream. Spread the remainder over the top and sides of the cake, swirling it decoratively with a palette knife.

For chocolate, toffee & pecan cake, add 75 g (3 oz) chopped pecan nuts to the cake mixture together with the ground almonds and cook as above. Omit the chocolate cream filling and topping and instead use a 500 g (1 lb) jar of dulce de leche (toffee caramel). Spread half in the centre of the cake and half on top. Decorate with 8 pecan halves.

mega chocolate roulade

Serves **8**
Preparation time **30 minutes**,
plus cooling
Cooking time **15 minutes**

175 g (6 oz) **plain dark
chocolate**
5 **eggs**, yolks and whites
separated
175 g (6 oz) **golden caster
sugar**, plus extra for
sprinkling
275 ml (9 fl oz) **double cream**
6 tablespoons ready-made
chocolate sauce
1 tablespoon **golden icing
sugar**, sieved
6 tablespoons ready-made
banoffee toffee
chocolate leaf shapes, to
decorate (see page 13)

Melt the chocolate in a bowl over a pan of simmering
water (see page 10). Whisk the egg yolks and caster
sugar in a bowl until pale and mousse-like. Whisk in
the melted chocolate.

Beat the egg whites in a separate bowl until they are
stiff. Use a large metal spoon to carefully fold one-
quarter of the whites into the chocolate mixture to
lighten it, then fold in the remainder.

Grease and line a 33 x 23 cm (13 x 9 inch) Swiss
roll tin. Turn the mixture into the tin, spreading right into
the corners. Bake in a preheated oven, 180°C (350°F),
Gas Mark 4, for 15 minutes until just firm to the touch.
Remove from the oven and cover with a damp clean
tea towel. Leave to cool for 1–2 hours.

Whip the cream until softly peaking, then stir in the
chocolate sauce, reserving 2 tablespoons. Stir in the
icing sugar.

Sprinkle a large piece of baking paper generously with
caster sugar. Turn out the roulade on to this. Spread
the banoffee toffee over the roulade to within 1 cm
(½ inch) of the edges, then spread over the chocolate
cream. Roll up, starting at a short end. Lift on to the
serving plate. Arrange the chocolate leaves on the top,
securing with the reserved chocolate cream.

For chocolate strawberry roulade, make the roulade
as above, but omit the banoffee cream filling. Instead,
fill with 5 tablespoons strawberry conserve, 250 g
(8 oz) mascarpone mixed with 2 tablespoons golden
caster sugar, and 50 g (2 oz) chopped strawberries.
Roll up the roulade and top with 4 halved strawberries.

chocolate mocha meringues

Makes **8**
Preparation time **15 minutes**,
  plus cooling
Cooking time **1 hour**

6 **egg whites**
350 g (11½ oz) **light
  muscovado sugar**
2 teaspoons **vanilla extract**
2 tablespoons **cornflour**
1 tablespoon **instant
  espresso coffee granules**
1 tablespoon **white wine
  vinegar**
75 g (3 oz) **plain dark
  chocolate**, broken into
  chunks
8 tablespoons **Greek yogurt**
8 teaspoons **runny honey**
8 **figs**

Whisk the egg whites in a grease-free bowl until they
are stiff. (Test if they are ready by upturning the bowl.
If the egg whites slide around, they need to be whisked
a little more; if they stay in place, they are ready.)

Whisk in the sugar 1 tablespoon at a time until it is
all mixed in. Mix together the vanilla extract, cornflour,
coffee granules and vinegar and fold into the meringue
along with the chocolate chunks.

Line a baking sheet with nonstick baking paper. Dollop
8 large spoonfuls of meringue on to the sheet. Bake
in a preheated oven, 150°C (300°F), Gas Mark 2, for
1 hour. Cool.

Serve the meringues on individual plates, each with a
spoonful of yogurt and a drizzle of honey. Cut a cross
in the top of each fig and gently squeeze it at the base
to open it up. Put 1 fig on each plate to finish.

For dark muscovado meringues, replace the
cornflour with 2 tablespoons cocoa powder
and prepare the meringues as above. Combine
4 tablespoons Greek yogurt with 4 tablespoons
whipped double cream, 1 tablespoon ginger syrup
and a pinch of ground ginger. Serve each meringue
with 1 tablespoon of this mixture and a piece of
stem ginger, cut into quarters.

chocolate nemesis & blueberries

Serves **12**
Preparation time **20 minutes**,
  plus cooling
Cooking time **30 minutes**

225 g (7½ oz) **golden caster
  sugar**
100 ml (3½ fl oz) **water**
325 g (11 oz) **plain dark
  chocolate**
225 g (7½ oz) **butter**
5 **eggs**
300 g (10 oz) **blueberries**,
  to serve
12 teaspoons **crème de
  cassis**, to serve

Heat 150 g (5 oz) sugar gently in a pan with the measured water until dissolved into a light syrup. Remove from the heat.

Melt the chocolate with the butter in a bowl over a pan of simmering water (see page 10). Pour the hot syrup into the melted chocolate, then remove from the heat.

Whisk the rest of the sugar together with the eggs until they are light and foamy and tripled in volume. Beat the chocolate into the whisked eggs slowly until well mixed in.

Grease a 23 cm (9 inch) springform cake tin and line with nonstick baking paper. Tip the mixture into the tin and rest the tin on a trivet in a roasting tin. Three-quarters fill the roasting tin with boiling water. Bake in a preheated oven, 120°C (250°F), Gas Mark ½, for 50 minutes until just firm.

Leave the cake to cool in the tin in the water. Serve in wedges with a few blueberries and a drizzle of crème de cassis.

For mocha amaretti nemesis, gently melt 200 g (7 oz) plain chocolate and 125 g (4 oz) milk chocolate with 225 g (7½ oz) butter and 3 tablespoons very strong espresso coffee. Sprinkle 150 g (5 oz) crumbled amaretti biscuits over the prepared tin, top with the melted chocolate mixture and bake as above. When cool, cut into wedges, dust with golden icing sugar and serve with 300 g (10 oz) raspberries. Drizzle 1 teaspoon Framboise around each portion.

chocolate fudge ring

Serves **12**
Preparation time **20 minutes**,
  plus cooling
Cooking time **40 minutes**

175 g (6 oz) **self-raising flour**
50 g (2 oz) **cocoa powder**
2 teaspoons **baking powder**
175 g (6 oz) **caster sugar**
175 g (6 oz) **butter**
4 **eggs**
2 teaspoons **vanilla essence**
4 tablespoons **milk**
walnut halves, to decorate

Icing
300 g (10 oz) **plain dark
  chocolate**, broken into
  pieces
4 tablespoons **milk**
50 g (2 oz) **butter**
225 g (7½ oz) **icing sugar**,
  plus extra for dusting

Sift the flour, cocoa powder and baking powder into a bowl. Add the sugar, butter, eggs, vanilla essence and milk and whisk until they are evenly combined.

Grease and line the base of a 1.8 litre (3 pint) ring cake tin. Turn the mixture into the tin and level the surface. Bake in a preheated oven, 180°C (350°F), Gas Mark 4, for 35 minutes or until just firm to the touch. Use a palette knife to loosen the cake from the side of the tin, then invert the cake on to a wire rack and leave to cool.

Heat the chocolate gently in a heavy-based pan with the milk until it has melted, stirring frequently. Stir in the butter. Beat in the icing sugar and leave the mixture to cool slightly.

Split the cake horizontally into 3 layers. Beat the icing again until it has a slightly fudge-like texture. Use a little icing to sandwich the layers together. Spread the remaining icing over the top and sides of the cake, swirling it with a palette knife. Decorate with the walnut halves and dust with icing sugar.

For chocolate walnut fudge ring, add 50 g (2 oz) finely chopped walnuts to the cake mixture. Serve with orange-flavoured crème fraîche, made by adding the finely grated rind of 1 orange to 200 g (7 oz) crème fraîche.

102

white chocolate & cranberry tarts

Makes **6**
Preparation time **30 minutes**,
  plus cooling and chilling
Cooking time **20 minutes**

250 g (8 oz) **frozen
  cranberries**
50 g (2 oz) **golden caster
  sugar**
4 tablespoons **crème de
  cassis**
200 g (7 oz) **creamy vanilla
  white chocolate**
300 g (10 oz) **fat-free
  fromage frais**
1 teaspoon **vanilla bean
  paste**
2 tablespoons **cranberry jelly**
6 ready-made **all-butter
  pastry cases**

Gently heat the cranberries, sugar and crème de cassis in a pan for a few minutes until the cranberries are just softened. Strain the cranberries and set aside to cool, reserving the juice.

Melt the white chocolate in a bowl over a pan of simmering water (see page 10). Stir in the fromage frais and vanilla bean paste and beat together well. Cover and chill.

Add the cranberry jelly to the reserved cranberry juice in the pan. Heat gently to melt the jelly and then stir to combine.

Spoon the vanilla and white chocolate mixture into the pastry cases 1–2 hours before serving. Top with the cranberries and spoon the cranberry syrup over to glaze. Chill until needed.

For homemade pastry cases, combine 175 g (6 oz) plain flour with 75 g (3 oz) butter until the mixture forms crumbs. Add 50 g (2 oz) icing sugar and 2 egg yolks and mix until a dough forms. Wrap in clingfilm and chill for 30 minutes. Grease and base-line 6 tins, 6 x 8 cm (2½ x 3¼ inch). Divide the pastry into 6, then press into the tins. Chill for 20 minutes. Trim off excess pastry, cover the pastry with nonstick baking paper, fill with baked beans and bake blind in a preheated oven, 190°C (375°F), Gas Mark 5, for 8 minutes. Remove the paper and beans and cook for 4 minutes until golden and crisp. Cool in the tins for 10 minutes, then cool on a wire rack before using.

very rich chocolate gateau

Serves **12–14**
Preparation time **25 minutes**,
  plus cooling and setting
Cooking time **40 minutes**

200 g (7 oz) **plain dark
  chocolate**
2 tablespoons **milk**
175 g (6 oz) **butter**
175 g (6 oz) **caster sugar**
175 g (6 oz) **ground
  hazelnuts** or **almonds**
40 g (1½ oz) **plain flour**
5 **eggs**, separated
3 tablespoons **hot water**

Syrup
25 g (1 oz) **caster sugar**
4 tablespoons **brandy** or
  orange/coffee liqueur
50 ml (2 fl oz) **water**

Glaze
5 tablespoons **apricot jam**
25 g (1 oz) **caster sugar**
75 ml (3 fl oz) **water**
200 g (7 oz) **plain dark
  chocolate**
25 g (1 oz) **milk chocolate**

Melt 200 g (7 oz) plain dark chocolate with the milk in a bowl over a pan of simmering water (see page 10). Put the chocolate mixture, butter, 175 g (6 oz) sugar, hazelnuts or almonds, flour and egg yolks in a bowl with the measured hot water and beat until smooth.

Whisk the egg whites until peaking, then fold them into the chocolate mixture.

Grease and line a 23 cm (9 inch) cake tin. Turn the mixture into the tin and level. Bake in a preheated oven, 180°C (350°F), Gas Mark 4, for about 30 minutes until just firm. Cover with a damp tea towel and leave to cool.

Mix 25 g (1 oz) sugar, the brandy or liqueur and measured water in a small pan and heat gently until the sugar dissolves. Boil rapidly for 1 minute until syrupy. Invert the cake on to a wire rack, remove the lining paper and spoon the syrup over the top.

Heat the apricot jam, press through a sieve and brush over the cake.

Heat 25 g (1 oz) caster sugar in a small, heavy-based pan with 75 ml (3 fl oz) water until the sugar has dissolved. Boil rapidly for 1 minute. Remove from the heat, leave for 1 minute, then stir in 200 g (7 oz) plain dark chocolate. Stir frequently until melted. Leave until beginning to thicken. Melt the milk chocolate.

Pour the chocolate glaze over the cake, easing it down the side with a palette knife. Drizzle the milk chocolate around the top edges of the cake to give a decorative finish. Leave in a cool place to set.

easy coconut & chocolate cakes

Makes **6**
Preparation time **20 minutes**,
  plus cooling
Cooking time **30 minutes**

75 g (3 oz) **sweetened
  shredded tenderized
  coconut**
175 g (6 oz) **self-raising flour**
1 teaspoon **baking powder**
175 g (6 oz) **golden caster
  sugar**
3 large **eggs**, lightly beaten
175 g (6 oz) **butter**, melted
200 g (7 oz) **milk chocolate**

Reserve one-third of the coconut and put the rest in a large bowl. Add the flour, baking powder, sugar, eggs and melted butter. Mix together well until smooth.

Grease and line the base of 8 heart-shaped moulds, approximately 5 cm (2 inch) in diameter. Spoon the mixture into the moulds and bake in a preheated oven, 180°C (350°F), Gas Mark 4, for 20 minutes until the cakes are risen and a skewer inserted into the centre comes out clean. Turn on to a wire rack to cool, placing the rack over a baking sheet.

Melt the chocolate in a bowl over a pan of simmering water (see page 10). Use a palette knife to spread the chocolate around the sides of the cakes, then pour the rest of the chocolate over the top of the cakes, allowing it to trickle down the sides.

Sprinkle over the reserved coconut to decorate and allow to set before serving.

For cranberry, choc chip & coconut cake, grease and line an 18 cm (7 inch) heart-shaped tin. Add 75 g (3 oz) each dried cranberries and milk chocolate chips and 2 tablespoons cranberry juice to the other cake mixture ingredients and continue as above. To finish, sprinkle 25 g (1 oz) dried cranberries over the chocolate and coconut decoration.

chocolate & fresh berry cakes

Makes **12**
Preparation time **20 minutes**,
  plus cooling
Cooking time **15 minutes**

125 g (4 oz) **butter**
125 g (4 oz) **light muscovado
  sugar**
2 **eggs**
100 g (3½ oz) **wholemeal
  self-raising flour**
1 tablespoon **cocoa powder**
2 tablespoons **milk**

Icing
100 g (3½ oz) **redcurrants**
300 g (10 oz) **golden icing
  sugar**
12 sprigs of 2–3 **redcurrants**,
  to decorate

Cream the butter and light muscovado sugar in a bowl until they are light and fluffy. Whisk in the eggs gradually, then sift in the flour and cocoa powder, tipping in the bran left in the sieve. Add the milk and gently fold everything together.

Line a patty tin with 12 paper cases. Divide the mixture among the cases and bake in a preheated oven at 200°C (400°F), Gas Mark 6, for 15 minutes until the cakes are risen and pale golden. Cool on a wire rack.

Remove the redcurrants from the stems with a fork and put them in a food processor. Whiz until smooth. Add half the golden icing sugar and whiz again until combined. Add the remaining golden icing sugar and blend again until smooth. Spoon the redcurrant icing on top of the cakes and finish each cake with a redcurrant sprig.

For white chocolate & raspberry cakes, use 75 g (3 oz) white chocolate chips instead of the cocoa. Replace the redcurrants in the icing with a good handful of raspberries. To finish, decorate each cake with 3 fresh whole raspberries.

the only birthday cake you need

Serves **12**
Preparation time **20 minutes**
Cooking time **20–25 minutes**

125 g (4 oz) **butter**
175 g (6 oz) **golden caster sugar**
175 g (6 oz) **light muscovado sugar**
2 **eggs**
225 g (7½ oz) **wholemeal self-raising flour**
50 g (2 oz) **cocoa powder**
¼ teaspoon **bicarbonate of soda**
250 ml (8 fl oz) **natural yogurt**

Icing
300 g (10 oz) **golden icing sugar**, sifted
2 tablespoons **cocoa powder**, sifted
15 g (½ oz) **butter**, melted
3–4 tablespoons **boiling water**

To decorate
150 g (5 oz) **milk** or **plain dark chocolate caraque** (see page 13)

Cream the butter, golden caster sugar and light muscovado sugar together in a bowl until light and fluffy. Add the eggs one at a time, beating well between each addition. Sift the flour, cocoa powder and bicarbonate of soda into the mixture, then tip in any bran left in the sieve. Pour in the natural yogurt. Stir everything together until smooth.

Grease and line the base of a 28 x 18 cm (11 x 7 inch) tin. Spoon the mixture into the tin and bake in a preheated oven at 180°C (350°F), Gas Mark 4, for 20–25 minutes until just firm and shrinking away from the sides of the tin and a skewer inserted into the centre comes out clean. Cool in the tin for 5 minutes, then turn on to a wire rack to cool completely.

Sift the icing sugar and cocoa powder into a bowl, then pour in the melted butter and 2 tablespoons boiling water. Stir to a smooth spreading consistency. If it is too stiff, very carefully add a little more boiling water, drop by drop. Spread the icing over the cake top, using a palette knife dipped in hot water. Wrap a ribbon around the sides and tie in a bow. Finish with the chocolate caraque and the birthday candles.

For personalized cake decoration, instead of the caraque, melt 75 g (3 oz) each milk and plain dark chocolate in separate bowls over pans of simmering water (see page 10). Spoon each type of melted chocolate into a piping bag and pipe simple shapes of your choice on top of the cake, such as hearts, whirls, flowers and lettering. You could also use white chocolate for additional colour contrast.

oh-so-easy almond torte

Serves **16**
Preparation time **20 minutes**,
  plus cooling
Cooking time 1¼ **hours**

200 g (7 oz) **plain dark
  chocolate**
5 large **eggs**
125 g (4 oz) **golden caster
  sugar**
100 g (3½ oz) **ground
  almonds**
1 tablespoon **coffee liqueur**
cocoa powder, for dusting
200 g (7 oz) fresh
  raspberries

Melt the chocolate in a bowl over a pan of simmering water (see page 10).

Separate all but one of the eggs, reserving the whites. Whisk the remaining whole egg, egg yolks and sugar in a bowl until the mixture is thick and pale and leaves a trail when the beaters are lifted.

Whisk in the melted chocolate slowly and then add the almonds. Clean the beaters and whisk the egg whites until softly peaking. Whisk one-quarter of the egg whites into the mix to loosen it, then fold in the rest.

Grease and line a round cake tin, 12 cm (5 inches) in diameter and 8 cm (3½ inches) deep, ensuring the nonstick baking paper comes about 7 cm (3 inches) above the tin. Pour the mixture into the tin and bake in a preheated oven, 160°C (325°F), Gas Mark 3, for 1–1¼ hours or until a skewer inserted into the centre of the cake comes out clean.

Make several holes in the cake while still hot and drizzle over the coffee liqueur. Cool in the tin for 30 minutes. To serve, place the cake on a stand, dust with cocoa powder, top with a pile of raspberries and wrap a wide ribbon around it.

For chocolate macadamia slice, add 50 g (2 oz) chopped macadamia nuts with the ground almonds. Bake as above, in a lined 1 kg (2 lb) loaf tin. Drizzle the cake with 1 tablespoon sherry instead of the coffee liqueur and slice to serve.

sachertorte

Serves **16**
Preparation time **50 minutes**,
   plus cooling
Cooking time **1¼ hours**

225 g (7½ oz) **plain dark
   chocolate**
175 g (6 oz) **butter**
175 g (6 oz) **golden caster
   sugar**
5 **eggs**, lightly beaten
125 g (4 oz) **wholemeal self-
   raising flour**, sifted
3 tablespoons **cocoa powder**
4 tablespoons **rum**
8 **golden chocolate buttons**,
   to decorate

Ganache
175 g (6 oz) **plain dark
   chocolate**
75 g (3 oz) **butter**
4 tablespoons **double cream**,
   warmed

Melt the chocolate in a bowl over a pan of simmering
water (see page 10).

Cream together the butter and sugar until they are
pale and fluffy. Gradually beat in the eggs, sifting in a
little flour and cocoa powder halfway. Fold in the rest of
the flour and cocoa. Pour in the melted chocolate and
add 2 tablespoons rum. Stir to combine.

Grease and line a 20 cm (8 inch) springform tin or
daisy tin. Pour the mixture into the tin and bake in
a preheated oven, 190°C (375°F), Gas Mark 5, for
30 minutes, then cover with foil and cook for a further
15 minutes. The cake is ready when a skewer inserted
in the centre comes out clean.

Cool in the tin for 30 minutes. Turn the cake on to a
wire rack to finish cooling, placed over a baking sheet.
Drizzle with the remainder of the rum.

Melt the chocolate for the ganache. Stir in the butter
and cream, then pour over the cake, using a palette
knife to help smooth it over. Decorate the top of the
cake with the golden chocolate buttons.

For almond sachertorte, fold in 125 g (4 oz) frozen
grated marzipan with the flour and the cocoa powder
as above. Replace the rum with 4 tablespoons
Amaretto di Saronno liqueur and proceed with
the rest of the recipe as above.

solid chocolate surprise eggs

Makes **2**

Preparation time **15 minutes**,
   plus drying and chilling

Cooking time **10 minutes**

2 large **eggs**

100 g (3½ oz) **white
chocolate**

100 g (3½ oz) **milk chocolate**

2 teaspoons **dulce de leche
(toffee caramel)**

Push a metal skewer into the top pointed end of each egg to make a hole, then pick away some of the shell until the hole is 1 cm (½ inch) in diameter. Tip out the contents of the egg into a bowl (you can use this for another recipe). Rinse the shell under cold running water then upturn to dry for 20 minutes, or 'blow dry' inside the eggs on a low setting of a hair dryer.

Melt the white and milk chocolate in separate bowls over pans of simmering water (see page 10). Upturn the eggs in the egg cups, so that the hole is at the top. Carefully pour half the melted white chocolate into each egg. Chill the eggs for 30 minutes.

Pipe or spoon the dulce de leche (toffee caramel) into each egg. Fill each egg with half the melted milk chocolate and chill for 2 hours until the chocolate is really firm.

Tap the egg shell gently to crack it and carefully peel away the shell, trying not to finger the chocolate too much. Place each egg in an egg cup. To eat your egg, run a knife under hot water, dry it, then slice the chocolate with the warm knife.

easter nest torte

Serves **12**

Preparation time **50 minutes**,
   plus cooling and chilling

Cooking time **25–30 minutes**

75 g (3 oz) **self-raising flour**
½ teaspoon **baking powder**
40 g (1½ oz) **cocoa powder**
125 g (4 oz) **butter**
125 g (4 oz) **caster sugar**
2 **eggs**
4 tablespoons **orange liqueur**
   or **orange juice**
75 g (3 oz) **plain dark**
   chocolate

Filling
2 teaspoons **gelatine**
2 tablespoons **cold water**
3 **egg yolks**
50 g (2 oz) **caster sugar**
1 teaspoon **cornflour**
300 ml (½ pint) **milk**
200 g (7 oz) **plain dark**
   chocolate, in pieces
300 ml (½ pint) **whipping cream**

To decorate
2 **flaky chocolate bars**,
   broken into shards
mini chocolate eggs

Sift the flour, baking powder and cocoa powder into a bowl. Add the butter, sugar and eggs and whisk until the mixture is smooth.

Grease a 23 cm (9 inch) springform or cake tin and line the base. Turn the mixture into the tin and bake in a preheated oven, 180°C (350°F), Gas Mark 4, for 20–25 minutes until just firm. Cool on a wire rack. Transfer to a serving plate and drizzle with the liqueur or juice.

Cut a strip of greaseproof paper 1 cm (½ inch) longer than the sponge circumference and 6 cm (2½ inches) deep. Melt the chocolate (see page 10) and spread it along the paper, to the edge on 1 long side and on the other in a slightly wavy line about 1.5 cm (¾ inch) from the edge. Leave 1 cm (½ inch) free of chocolate at 1 end. Set aside for 15 minutes, then lift the paper and secure it around the sponge so the straight edge rests on the plate and the ends meet. Chill.

Sprinkle the gelatine over the measured water and leave to soften. Beat the egg yolks in a bowl with the sugar, cornflour and a little milk. Bring the remaining milk to the boil. Pour it over the egg yolk mix, whisking. Return to the pan and cook gently until thickened.

Remove from the heat and stir in the gelatine until dissolved. Add 200 g (7 oz) chocolate and leave until melted. Stir smooth, then leave to cool until thickening.

Whip the cream to peaks and fold into the chocolate mix. Turn into the case on top of the sponge and level. Chill for 1–2 hours until set. Remove the paper strip. Lay the chocolate shards on top to create a nest. Pile the mini eggs in the centre. Chill until ready to serve.

bûche de noël

Serves **10**
Preparation time **40 minutes**,
  plus cooling
Cooking time **20 minutes**

3 eggs
75 g (3 oz) **caster sugar**,
  plus extra for sprinkling
50 g (2 oz) **plain flour**, sifted
25 g (1 oz) **cocoa powder**,
  sifted

Filling
150 ml (¼ pint) **double cream**
150 g (5 oz) canned
  sweetened chestnut purée

Chocolate cream
150 ml (¼ pint) **double cream**
200 g (7 oz) **plain dark
  chocolate**, broken into
  pieces

To decorate
3 **flaky chocolate bars**
icing sugar, for dusting

Whisk the eggs and sugar in a bowl over a pan of hot water until the mix leaves a trail when the beaters are lifted. Fold the flour and cocoa powder into the mixture until just combined. Spread into the tin.

Grease and line a 33 x 23 cm (13 x 9 inch) Swiss roll tin and bake in a preheated oven, 180°C (350°F), Gas Mark 4, for about 15 minutes until just firm. Sprinkle a sheet of nonstick baking paper with caster sugar and invert the cake on to it. Peel away the lining paper, then roll the sponge up in the fresh paper and leave to cool.

Whip the cream until softly peaking, then fold in the chestnut purée. Unroll the sponge and spread the chestnut cream over the top. Roll the cake back up.

Bring the cream almost to the boil in a small pan. Remove from the heat and stir in the chocolate. Leave until melted, then stir until smooth. Cool.

Place the cake join side down on a serving plate. Lightly whip the chocolate cream to thicken slightly, then spread over the cake, leaving the ends exposed. Cut the flaky bar lengthways into long pieces. Press them lightly on to the chocolate cream to decorate, filling in the gaps with smaller pieces. Dust the log generously with icing sugar and serve.

For brandy butter roll, omit the chestnut filling and instead use 125 g (4 oz) brandy butter mixed with 150 ml (¼ pint) crème fraîche. Dust with cocoa instead of icing sugar. Serve with a sauce made by mixing 2 teaspoons arrowroot with 1 tablespoon cold water and adding to 150 ml (¼ pint) warmed mulled wine. Heat the sauce until it is thickened and clear.

heavenly christmas cake

Serves **20**

Preparation time **1 hour**, plus
soaking fruit and cooling

Cooking time **1¾ hours**

250 g (8 oz) **dried fruit**
200 ml (7 fl oz) **sherry**
250 g (8 oz) **butter**
225 g (7½ oz) **molasses
sugar**
3 **eggs**
200 g (7 oz) **self-raising
wholemeal flour**
50 g (2 oz) **cocoa powder**
2 tablespoons **mixed spice**
4 pieces **stem ginger**,
chopped
100 g (3½ oz) **white
chocolate**, chopped

To decorate
150 g (5 oz) **butter**
150 g (5 oz) **golden icing
sugar**
150 g (5 oz) **cream cheese**
1 tablespoon **brandy**
125 g (4 oz) **dried
cranberries**

Seal the dried fruit and sherry in a sterilized jar
(see page 11) and leave to macerate for at least
1 hour and up to 1 week.

Cream the butter and sugar until fluffy. Gradually
add the eggs, then sift in the flour, cocoa, mixed spice
and ginger.

Whiz half the macerated fruit in a processor until
smooth. Add to the cake mixture with the rest of the
fruit and alcoholic liquid. Add the white chocolate and
fold everything together.

Grease and line a 15 cm (6 inch) cake tin. Spoon the
mixture into the tin and bake in a preheated oven,
180°C (350°F), Gas Mark 4, for 1½ hours. The cake is
ready when a skewer pushed in the centre comes out
clean. Cool in the tin. Put on to a plate or board and
peel away the lining paper.

Blend the butter, sugar, cream cheese and brandy
together in a food processor until smooth and spread
on top of the cake. Finish by decorating with dried
cranberries and tying a large ribbon around the sides.

For classic marzipan & icing decoration, instead of
brandy frosting, brush the top and sides of the cooled
cake with 4 tablespoons apricot glaze. Roll out 500 g
(1 lb) natural marzipan to a 25 cm (10 inch) circle,
then position on the cake, press in place and trim off
any excess. Mix 3 egg whites in a large bowl, then
beat in 500 g (1 lb) sieved golden icing sugar until
stiff. Add 1 teaspoon glycerine. Use a palette knife to
spread the icing over the cake. Leave to set before
decorating with the cranberries.

kids'
favourites

chocolate hazelnut spread

Makes **500 g (1 lb)**
Preparation time **10 minutes**,
  plus cooling
Cooking time **5 minutes**

375 g (12 oz) **milk chocolate**
125 g (4 oz) **hazelnuts**
2 tablespoons **vegetable oil**
2 tablespoons **golden caster
  sugar**
1 tablespoon **cocoa powder**
½ teaspoon **vanilla extract**

Sterilize a 400 g (13 oz) glass jar (see page 11), then melt the chocolate in a bowl over a pan of simmering water (see page 10).

Grind the hazelnuts into a paste in a food processor. Add the oil, sugar, cocoa powder and vanilla extract and whiz again, to combine.

Pour in the melted chocolate and blend until the mixture is very smooth, warm and runny. Pour it into the sterilized jar and cover. Leave to cool and thicken slightly before using. It will keep for up to 1 month, covered, at room temperature.

For milk & white chocolate spread, melt the milk chocolate as above, then finely chop 125 g (4 oz) white chocolate in a food processor. Omit the hazelnuts and proceed as above, adding the oil, caster sugar, cocoa powder and vanilla extract to the food processor, then the melted milk chocolate.

chocolate caramel shortbread

Makes **20**
Preparation time **25 minutes**,
  plus cooling and setting
Cooking time **40 minutes**

200 g (7 oz) **plain flour**
50 g (2 oz) **cocoa powder**
75 g (3 oz) **golden caster
  sugar**
175 g (6 oz) **butter**
200 g (7 oz) **white chocolate**

Caramel
750 g (1½ lb) **condensed
  milk**
100 g (3½ oz) **light
  muscovado sugar**
100 g (3½ oz) **butter**

Blend the flour, cocoa powder, sugar and butter in a food processor until the mixture forms crumbs, then pulse a little more until it forms a ball. Turn on to a lightly floured surface and knead until it is smooth and well combined.

Grease and line a 30 x 20 cm (12 x 8 inch) Swiss roll tin. Press the mixture into the tin and bake in a preheated oven, 180°C (350°F), Gas Mark 4, for 20 minutes until firm to the touch.

Heat the condensed milk, sugar and butter in a nonstick pan, stirring continuously, for about 15 minutes until the mixture is thick and fudgy. Pour on top of the chocolate shortbread, smooth over and cool.

Melt the white chocolate in a bowl over a pan of simmering water (see page 10) and pour it over the caramel. Leave to set at room temperature, then cut into 20 squares.

For dark chocolate shortbread, omit the caramel ingredients and prepare a base mixture as above using 125 g (4 oz) plain flour, 75 g (3 oz) ground rice, 50 g (2 oz) cocoa, 75 g (3 oz) light muscovado sugar and 175 g (6 oz) butter. Press into a greased 20 cm (8 in) round tin. Mark out 8 triangles, fork the edges to decorate and bake as above. Dust with golden caster sugar to serve.

serious chocolate pancakes

Serves **4**
Preparation time **5 minutes**
Cooking time **10 minutes**

100 g (3½ oz) **plain flour**,
  sifted
1 tablespoon **cocoa powder**
1 **egg**
300 ml (½ pint) **milk**
sunflower oil, for frying
1 **chocolate honeycomb bar**,
  chopped
75 g (3 oz) **butter**
75 g (3 oz) **golden caster
  sugar**
rind of 1 **orange**, finely grated
4 tablespoons **orange juice**

Put the flour, cocoa powder, egg and milk into a food processor and blend to a smooth batter. Pour the batter into a jug and heat the oil in a 23 cm (9 inch) nonstick pan. Add 100 ml (3½ fl oz) batter to the pan, swirling it around to completely cover the base.

Cook the pancake for 1–2 minutes until pale golden on the underside, then turn it over and fry the other side. Tip on to a plate and repeat 3 more times with the batter to make 4 pancakes, interleaving them with nonstick baking paper as they pile up on the plate.

Put a few pieces of chocolate honeycomb bar into the centre of each pancake and fold in all 4 sides to make a rectangle.

Heat the butter and sugar in the frying pan and when the sugar has dissolved, add the orange rind and juice and slip in the pancakes. Warm through for 3 minutes. Serve the pancakes drenched in the orange sauce.

For chocolate ice cream pancakes, make the pancakes as above but fill each one with a dollop of toffee ice cream instead of the honeycomb bar pieces. Omit the orange sauce and instead heat 2 chopped large caramel chocolate bars very gently in a small heavy-based saucepan. When melted, stir well and serve at once over the pancakes.

chocolate muffins

Makes **12**
Preparation time **15 minutes**
Cooking time **25 minutes**

375 g (12 oz) **self-raising flour**
25 g (1 oz) **cocoa powder**
200 g (7 oz) **golden caster sugar**
2 large **eggs**
150 ml (¼ pint) **sunflower oil**
150 ml (¼ pint) **milk**
1 teaspoon **vanilla extract**
12 teaspoons ready-made **chocolate spread** or homemade **Chocolate Hazelnut Spread** (see page 128)

Sieve the flour and cocoa powder into a bowl and add the sugar, stirring to mix.

Combine the eggs, sunflower oil, milk and vanilla extract in a jug, using a fork. Pour the wet ingredients into the dry and stir a few times until the ingredients are just combined.

Line a 12-hole muffin tin with paper cases. Half-fill the cases with muffin mixture, add 1 teaspoon chocolate spread to each case and then top with the rest of the muffin mixture.

Bake in a preheated oven, 190°C (375°F), Gas Mark 5, for 25 minutes until the muffins are well risen and springy to the touch.

For orange & chocolate doughnut muffins, omit the cocoa and replace it with 25 g (1 oz) cornflour. Leave out the vanilla extract, add the finely grated rind of 1 orange and 1 tablespoon grape juice, then proceed with the recipe as above. When cooked, brush the muffin tops with 25 g (1 oz) melted butter and dredge with golden caster sugar.

chocolate rice crispy rings

Makes **10**
Preparation time **10 minutes**
Cooking time **5 minutes**

150 g (5 oz) **chewy toffees**
2 tablespoons **cocoa powder**
50 g (2 oz) **butter**
200 g (7 oz) **marshmallows**
175 g (6 oz) **rice crispies**

Place the chewy toffees into a large microwave-safe bowl with the cocoa powder and butter. Microwave on high (900 watts) for 3 minutes. Carefully remove the bowl from the microwave using oven gloves. Alternatively, melt the toffees with the cocoa powder and butter in pan over a gentle heat. Stir the mixture with a wooden spoon, then tip in the marshmallows (there is no need to stir again at this stage).

Microwave on high (900 watts) or return the pan to the heat for 1 minute, then stir quickly to mix. Add one-third of the rice crispies and mix them into the toffee mixture. Add the rest of the rice crispies in 2 batches, stirring well after each addition.

Grease a 10 cm (4 inch) ring (rum baba) mould. Take a handful of the rice crispie mixture and press it into the mould to make a ring shape. Press it down firmly with the palm of your hand, then twist and upturn it to release it from the mould. Place it on a sheet of nonstick baking paper. Repeat with the rest of the mixture to make 10 rings in all. To decorate, press white bows on to the mixture (optional). Allow to set before serving.

For white chocolate rice crispy bars, omit the cocoa powder and combine the rest of the ingredients as above. Spoon the mixture into a 17 x 28 cm (7 x 11 inch) tin. Melt 100 g (3½ oz) white chocolate (see page 10) and pour on top. Allow to set, then cut into bars to serve.

banana & chocolate ring

Serves **12**
Preparation time **20 minutes**,
  plus cooling
Cooking time **1 hour**

200 g (7 oz) **plain dark
  chocolate**
175 g (6 oz) **butter**
250 g (8 oz) **self-raising
  flour**, sifted
1 teaspoon **baking powder**
150 g (5 oz) **light muscovado
  sugar**
rind of 1 **lemon**, finely grated
3 **eggs**
150 g (5 oz) **white chocolate**,
  broken into pieces
3 small **bananas**, mashed
200 g (5 oz) **white chocolate**,
  broken into pieces
125 g (4 oz) **white chocolate
  chips**

Melt the chocolate with 25 g (1 oz) of the butter in a bowl over a pan of simmering water (see page 10).

Cut the rest of the butter into small cubes, mix with the the flour and baking powder in a food processor and blend to crumbs. Add the sugar, lemon rind, eggs, white chocolate and bananas. Whiz until well combined.

Grease a 1.8 litre (3 pint) ring tin. Line the base and sides with nonstick baking paper. Spoon one-quarter of the cake mixture into the base, then drizzle over one-third of the chocolate. Continue layering the cake mixture and chocolate, finishing with cake mixture.

Bake in a preheated oven, 180°C (350°F), Gas Mark 4, for 50–60 minutes until the cake feels firm when lightly pressed. Leave in the tin for 10 minutes, then loosen the edges with a knife and turn out on to a wire rack to cool.

Melt the white chocolate in a pan over a bowl of simmering water. Drizzle over the top of the cake. Decorate with the white chocolate chips.

For banana, chocolate & pecan ring, replace the white chocolate in the cake with 150 g (5 oz) milk chocolate and the lemon rind with 50 g (2 oz) finely chopped pecan nuts. Instead of topping with white chocolate, make a ganache. Bring 150 ml (¼ pint) double cream to the boil in a small pan, remove from the heat and add 200 g (7 oz) plain dark chocolate, broken into pieces. Stir to melt the chocolate and make a smooth, thick sauce. Pour the ganache over the cake and finish with pecan halves.

white choc & coconut mini muffins

Makes **24**
Preparation time **15 minutes**
Cooking time **8 minutes**

150 g (5 oz) **self-raising flour**
½ teaspoon **bicarbonate of soda**
75 g (3 oz) **golden caster sugar**
50 g (2 oz) **sweetened tenderized shredded coconut**
50 g (2 oz) **white chocolate chips**
150 ml (¼ pint) **vanilla-flavoured yogurt**
1 **egg**
4 tablespoons **sunflower oil**

To decorate
3 tablespoons **strawberry jam**
3 tablespoons **sweetened tenderized shredded coconut**

Sift the flour and bicarbonate of soda into a bowl. Add the sugar, coconut and white chocolate chips.

Mix the yogurt, egg and sunflower oil together in a jug, using a fork. Pour the wet ingredients into the dry and gently mix everything together.

Line 24 mini muffin tins with paper mini muffin cases. Spoon the mixture into the muffin cases and bake in a preheated oven, 190°C (375°F), Gas Mark 5, for 6–8 minutes until the muffins are well risen and firm.

Brush over the strawberry jam while the muffins are still warm, and sprinkle over the coconut.

For snowcap coconut mini muffins, decorate the muffins with 100 g (3½ oz) melted white chocolate, spooned on top of the cooled muffins. Omit the shredded coconut and instead sprinkle over 3 tablespoons white chocolate chips to finish.

chocolate cherry patties

Makes **12**
Preparation time **15 minutes**,
  plus cooling
Cooking time **25 minutes**

175 g (6 oz) **butter**
150 g (5 oz) **ground almonds**
150 g (5 oz) **caster sugar**
40 g (1½ oz) **plain flour**
4 **egg whites**
100 g (3½ oz) **plain dark
  chocolate**, coarsely grated
425 g (14 oz) **black or red
  cherries**, pitted, in syrup,
  thoroughly drained
icing sugar, for dusting

Melt the butter and leave to cool slightly.

Mix together the almonds, sugar and flour in a bowl.
Add the egg whites, melted butter and chocolate, and
mix until they are evenly combined.

Grease lightly a 12-hole muffin tin. Spoon the muffin
mixture into the holes and arrange 3 cherries on top
of each patty.

Bake in a preheated oven, 200°C (400°F), Gas Mark
6, for about 20 minutes until risen, golden and just firm
in the centre. Leave in the tin for 10 minutes, then
transfer to a wire rack to cool.

Dust lightly with icing sugar to serve.

For chocolate, walnut & pear patties, replace the
ground almonds with 150 g (5 oz) walnuts, finely
ground in a food processor. Finely slice the contents
of a 425 g (14 oz) can of pears and arrange the
pieces on top of the cakes in place of the cherries
before baking as above.

ice cream birthday cake

Serves **12**
Preparation time **20 minutes**,
plus freezing

1.5 litres (2½ pints) **chocolate
fudge brownie ice cream**
500 ml (17 fl oz) **strawberry
cheesecake ice cream**
milk chocolate curls (see
page 12)

Remove the ice cream from the freezer, to allow
it to soften up slightly. Base-line a 23 cm (9 inch)
springform tin with nonstick baking paper. Tip two-
thirds of the chocolate ice cream into the lined tin
and spread around evenly using a palette knife.

Spread over the strawberry ice cream in the same way,
then top with the remainder of the chocolate ice cream.
Replace on a flat surface in the freezer.

Take the ice cream cake out of the freezer just before
the party and place on a serving plate. Decorate with
chocolate curls. Then carefully replace in the freezer,
until ready to serve. Push in some candles before
serving, if wished.

For Neapolitan ice cream birthday cake, layer
500 ml (17 fl oz) vanilla ice cream, 500 ml (17 fl oz)
strawberry cheesecake yogurt ice cream and 500 ml
(17 fl oz) chocolate fudge brownie ice cream in the
tin. Decorate with chocolate curls and 12 whole
strawberries and freeze as above.

mega choc chip berry cookies

Makes **8**
Preparation time **15 minutes**,
  plus chilling
Cooking time **15 minutes**

125 g (4 oz) **butter**
125 g (4 oz) **light muscovado
  sugar**
2 **eggs**, lightly beaten
2 teaspoons **vanilla extract**
225 g (7½ oz) **wholemeal
  self-raising flour**
25 g (1 oz) **cocoa powder**
75 g (3 oz) **dried cranberries**
100 g (3½ oz) **white
  chocolate**, roughly chopped
100 g (3½ oz) **milk chocolate**,
  roughly chopped
8 **walnut halves** or **pecan
  halves**

Mix the butter and sugar together in a bowl using a wooden spoon until soft and fluffy. Gradually beat in the eggs and vanilla extract.

Sift in the flour and cocoa powder and add the cranberries and chocolate. Mix the dough together with your hands. Knead lightly, then wrap in clingfilm and chill for at least 30 minutes.

Cover 2 baking sheets with nonstick baking paper. Roll the mixture into 8 balls and arrange, well spaced apart, on the paper. Flatten each one with the heel of your hand and top with a walnut or pecan half.

Bake in a preheated oven, 180°C (350°F), Gas Mark 4, for 15 minutes until just firm. Leave on the tray for 5 minutes to firm up slightly and serve while warm. Alternatively, cool on a wire rack, then store in an airtight container.

For vanilla, blueberry & chocolate chip cookies, beat together the butter, sugar, eggs and vanilla extract as above, then sift in 275 g (9 oz) wholemeal self-raising flour and 75 g (3 oz) dried blueberries. Mix the dough and chill before shaping and baking as above, omitting the walnut or pecan halves decoration.

chocolate cornflake bars

Makes **12**
Preparation time **10 minutes**,
  plus chilling
Cooking time **3 minutes**

200 g (7 oz) **milk chocolate**,
  broken into pieces
2 tablespoons **golden syrup**
50 g (2 oz) **olive oil spread**
125 g (4 oz) **cornflakes**

Melt the chocolate with the golden syrup and olive oil spread in a bowl over a pan of simmering water (see page 10).

Stir in the cornflakes and mix well together.

Grease a 28 x 18 cm (11 x 7 inch) tin. Turn the mixture into the tin, chill until set, then cut into 12 bars.

For crunchy muesli & apricot cakes, replace the cornflakes with 125 g (4 oz) muesli and 50 g (2 oz) chopped dried apricots. Combine with the chocolate mixture, spoon into 12 paper cake cases and chill until set.

mini chocolate meringues

Makes **6**
Preparation time **15 minutes**
Cooking time **1¼ hours**

3 **egg whites**
75 g (3 oz) **golden caster sugar**
75 g (3 oz) **light muscovado sugar**
75 g (3 oz) **milk chocolate**, grated

Whisk the egg whites in a grease-free bowl until stiffly peaking. Whisk in the golden caster sugar 1 tablespoon at a time, then whisk in the light muscovado sugar, also 1 tablespoon at a time. Fold in the chocolate.

Line 2 baking sheets with nonstick baking paper. Drop teaspoonfuls of the meringue mixture on to the baking sheets.

Bake in a preheated oven to 140°C (275°F), Gas Mark 1, for 1¼ hours, then turn off the heat and leave in the oven for another 30 minutes. These meringues go well with strawberries and Triple Chocolate Fondue (see page 234).

For mini chocolate vacherin, make up the meringue as above, but use 150 g (5 oz) golden caster sugar instead of the mixed caster and muscovado sugar. Fold in 75 g (3 oz) grated white chocolate in place of the milk chocolate. Flatten teaspoonfuls of the mixture on lined baking sheets to make thin discs, then bake as above. Serve each pair sandwiched with 1 teaspoon each strawberry jam and strained Greek yogurt and 2 slices of fresh peach.

neapolitan whirl ice cream

Serves **8**
Preparation time **20 minutes**,
  plus cooling and freezing
Cooking time **5 minutes**

225 g (7½ oz) **raspberries**
175 g (6 oz) **caster sugar**
150 ml (¼ pint) **water**
200 g (7 oz) **plain dark
  chocolate**
600 ml (1 pint) **double cream**

Press the raspberries through a sieve to make a purée. Heat the sugar and measured water in a pan until the sugar dissolves. Bring to the boil and boil for 2 minutes until syrupy. Leave to cool.

Melt the chocolate with 150 ml (¼ pint) of the cream in a bowl over a pan of simmering water (see page 10). Stir until smooth, then allow to cool slightly. Whip the remaining cream with the cooled syrup until the mixture is softly peaking.

Spoon half the cream and syrup mixture into a separate bowl and fold in the raspberry purée. Half-fold the chocolate mixture into the remaining cream and syrup mixture until marbled.

Put alternate spoonfuls of the raspberry and chocolate mixtures in a freezer container. Using a large metal spoon, fold the mixtures together 2 or 3 times until slightly mingled. Freeze overnight until firm.

Transfer the ice cream to the refrigerator about 30 minutes before serving. Serve scooped into bowls.

For strawberry yogurt ice cream, whiz 225 g (7½ oz) strawberries in a blender until they make a smooth purée. Melt the chocolate with 150 ml (¼ pint) double cream and fold it into 300 ml (½ pint) strained Greek yogurt. Add alternate spoonfuls of the strawberry purée and chocolate yogurt mix, fold together and freeze as above.

chewy nutty chocolate brownies

Makes **15**
Preparation time **10 minutes**,
  plus cooling
Cooking time **30 minutes**

75 g (3 oz) **plain dark**
  chocolate
100 g (3½ oz) **butter**
200 g (7 oz) **soft light brown**
  sugar
2 **eggs**, beaten
few drops **vanilla extract**
50 g (2 oz) **ground almonds**
25 g (1 oz) **cornmeal** or
  polenta
150 g (5 oz) mixed **nuts**,
  toasted and roughly
  chopped
ice cream, to serve (optional)

Melt the chocolate with the butter in a bowl over a pan of simmering water (see page 10).

Stir in all the remaining ingredients and combine well.

Grease and line a 28 x 18 cm (11 x 7 inch) baking tin. Turn the mixture into the tin and bake in a preheated oven, 180°C (350°F) Gas Mark 4, for 30 minutes until slightly springy in the centre.

Remove from the oven and cool for 10 minutes in the tin, then cut into 15 squares. Serve with ice cream, if liked.

For coffee custard sauce, to serve with the brownies, heat 300 ml (½ pint) each milk and cream with 25 g (1 oz) instant coffee granules and bring to the boil. Whisk 4 egg yolks and 75 g (3 oz) golden caster sugar in a bowl until thick and creamy. Slowly pour on the hot milk, whisking all the time. Return to the pan and stir gently over a low heat until the mixture thickens and coats the back of a spoon. Strain and serve hot or cold.

goodies & gifts

liqueur truffles

Makes **12**
Preparation time **50 minutes,**
 plus chilling
Cooking time **2 minutes**

200 g (7 oz) **plain dark
 chocolate**
150 ml (¼ pint) **double cream**
25 g (1 oz) **butter**
1 tablespoon **cream liqueur**
1 tablespoon **coffee liqueur**
12 **chocolate coffee beans**
300 g (10 oz) **milk chocolate**

Melt the plain dark chocolate in a bowl over a pan of simmering water (see page 10). Heat the cream until it reaches boiling point, then remove from the heat. Add the butter to the melted chocolate and stir until combined, then stir in the cream.

Divide the chocolate into 2 rectangular sealable containers. Add the cream liqueur to one container and the coffee liqueur to the other and mix each in well. Chill for at least 2 hours until firm.

Use a melon baller or 2 teaspoons to scoop out 6 cream liqueur truffles and arrange them on a paper-lined nonstick baking sheet. Repeat with the coffee liqueur truffles.

Melt the milk chocolate in a bowl over a pan of simmering water. Stir well, then, holding 1 truffle at a time on a fork over the bowl, spoon melted chocolate over the top to coat it. Place each truffle on a piece of waxed paper on a nonstick baking sheet. Press a chocolate coffee bean into the top of each truffle.

Leave the truffles for at least 1 hour, until the coating has set. Put them in petit-four cases and pack into a gift box or tin.

For white chocolate liqueur truffles, use 200 g (7 oz) white chocolate instead of the plain dark chocolate to make the truffles. Melt 200 g (7 oz) white chocolate cake covering with 100 g (3½ oz) white chocolate squares in a bowl over a pan of simmering water, and use to coat the truffles as described above.

double chocolate truffles

Makes **24**
Preparation time **45 minutes**,
  plus chilling
Cooking time **8 minutes**

250 ml (8 fl oz) **double cream**
200 g (7 oz) **plain dark
  chocolate**
3–4 tablespoons **brandy** or
  rum
2 tablespoons **cocoa powder**,
  sifted
200 g (7 oz) **plain dark
  chocolate**
crystallized violets

Pour the cream into a small pan and bring to the boil. Take the pan off the heat and break in 200 g (7 oz) plain dark chocolate. Leave to stand until it has melted, then stir in the brandy or rum and mix until smooth. Chill for 4 hours until the truffle mixture is firm.

Line a baking sheet with waxed paper and dust with cocoa powder. Scoop a little truffle mixture on to a teaspoon, then transfer it to a second spoon and back to the first again, making a well-rounded egg shape (or use a melon baller). Slide the truffle on to the cocoa-dusted paper. Repeat until all the mixture is used up. Chill again for 2 hours, or overnight if possible, until firm.

Melt 200 g (7 oz) plain dark chocolate in a bowl over a pan of simmering water (see page 10). Stir well, then, holding 1 truffle at a time on a fork over the bowl, spoon melted chocolate over the top to coat it. Place the truffles on a piece of waxed paper on a nonstick baking sheet. Swirl a little chocolate over the top of each with a spoon and finish with a crystallized violet.

Chill for at least 1 hour, then pack into petit-four cases and arrange in a gift box lined with purple tissue paper.

For minted mixed truffles, add 3–4 tablespoons mint liqueur to the chocolate truffle mix instead of the brandy or rum. Coat the truffles as described above, using 200 g (7 oz) melted milk chocolate instead of the plain dark chocolate.

cookies & cream fudge

Makes **36 pieces**
Preparation time **10 minutes**,
  plus cooling and chilling
Cooking time **15 minutes**

125 g (4 oz) **butter**
200 ml (7 fl oz) **evaporated
  milk**
450 g (14½ oz) **golden caster
  sugar**
50 ml (2 fl oz) **water**
2 teaspoons **vanilla extract**
75 g (3 oz) **plain dark
  chocolate**, chopped
1 teaspoon **vegetable oil**
8 **Oreo cookies or bourbon
  biscuits**, chopped

Heat the butter, evaporated milk, caster sugar, vanilla extract and measured water gently together in a heavy-based pan, stirring until the sugar has dissolved. Bring to the boil.

Boil the mixture for 10 minutes, stirring all the time (test to see if it is ready by carefully dropping ½ teaspoon of the mixture into some cold water – it should form a soft ball). Pour half the fudge mixture quickly into a heatproof jug. Add the chocolate to the pan and stir to melt.

Grease a 500 g (1 lb) loaf tin with the vegetable oil. Pour half the chocolate fudge into the base of the loaf tin, then carefully scatter over half the biscuits. Pour the vanilla fudge on top and scatter over the remainder of the biscuits. Finish with a final layer of chocolate fudge. Cool, cover with clingfilm and chill overnight.

Turn out the fudge on to a board and cut into pieces.

For chocolate orange fudge, prepare the fudge mixture as above, stirring in 75 g (3 oz) orange-flavoured dark chocolate, a pinch of ground cinnamon and a grating of nutmeg in place of the plain dark chocolate. Omit the Oreo cookies or bourbon biscuits and instead scatter chopped chocolate orange biscuits such as Jaffa Cakes over the first fudge layer.

rocky road clusters

Makes **28**
Preparation time **40 minutes**,
  plus cooling, chilling and
  setting
Cooking time **10 minutes**

150 g (5 oz) **mixed whole
  nuts** (such as cashews,
  hazelnuts, pistachios)
300 g (10 oz) **plain dark
  chocolate**
15 g (½ oz) **butter**
2 tablespoons **golden icing
  sugar**
2 tablespoons **double cream**

Toast the nuts on a piece of foil on a baking sheet under a preheated hot grill for 3–4 minutes until golden. Allow to cool slightly, then chop roughly.

Melt 75 g (3 oz) of the chocolate in a bowl over a pan of simmering water (see page 10). Stir the butter, sugar and cream into the melted chocolate until smooth and glossy, then mix in all but 2 tablespoons of the nuts. Drop rough teaspoons of the mixture on to a baking sheet lined with nonstick baking paper. Chill for 2–3 hours until firm.

Melt the remaining chocolate. Coat the nut clusters in the melted chocolate by holding them on a fork, one at a time, over the bowl of chocolate and spooning it over the top with a teaspoon. When the excess chocolate has dripped away from each cluster, return it to the paper-lined sheet.

Place the clusters in a cool place and leave to set for at least 1 hour. Sprinkle with the reserved nuts. Transfer them to petit-four cases when ready to serve.

For white chocolate clusters, toast only 125 g (4 oz) mixed whole nuts. Melt 75 g (3 oz) white chocolate and stir in the butter, icing sugar, cream and toasted nuts as above. Drop spoonfuls of the mixture on to a baking sheet, chill and dust with 2 tablespoons sieved golden icing sugar to serve.

peppermint white chocolate hearts

Makes **8**

Preparation time **10 minutes,** plus chilling

Cooking time **2 minutes**

200 g (7 oz) **white chocolate**
½ teaspoon **peppermint extract**

Melt the chocolate in a bowl over a pan of simmering water (see page 10) until just softened. Add the peppermint extract and stir together well.

Spoon the chocolate into 8 holes of a flexible ice-cube tray with heart-shaped moulds. Carefully place in the refrigerator and chill for at least 1 hour.

Line a baking sheet with nonstick paper. Upturn the ice-cube tray, then press the base of each heart to pop out the chocolates on to the sheet.

For spiced orange milk chocolate hearts, melt 200 g (7 oz) milk chocolate instead of the white chocolate. Omit the peppermint extract and stir in ¼ teaspoon ground mixed spice together with 2 teaspoons finely grated orange rind. Chill in an ice-cube tray as above.

boozy ginger chocs

Makes **12**
Preparation time **20 minutes**,
  plus freezing
Cooking time **5 minutes**

3 pieces of **stem ginger**,
  drained
1 tablespoon **Southern
  Comfort**
200 g (7 oz) **plain dark
  chocolate**, flavoured with
  orange and spices

Polish a flexible ice-cube tray with at least 12 sections using kitchen roll, then place in the freezer.

Cut each piece of stem ginger into quarters and place in a small bowl with the Southern Comfort.

Melt the chocolate in a bowl over a pan of simmering water (see page 10). Spoon the melted chocolate into each section of the ice-cube tray to half-fill it. Add a piece of macerated stem ginger, then pour the rest of the melted chocolate on top. Return to the freezer for 30 minutes.

Turn out the chocolates on to a piece of waxed paper to serve. Alternatively, chill in the refrigerator until you are ready to serve.

For boozy mint chocs, replace the ginger pieces with a handful of mint leaves and the Southern Comfort with 1 tablespoon brandy. Put a small mint leaf in the base of each section of the ice-cube tray, cutting to size if necessary. Add 1 tablespoon chopped mint to the melted chocolate with the brandy.

glazed chocolate ginger hearts

Makes **24**
Preparation time **30 minutes**,
   plus chilling and setting
Cooking time **15 minutes**

125 g (4 oz) **butter**
125 g (4 oz) **caster sugar**
1 **egg**
125 g (4 oz) **black treacle**
400 g (13 oz) **self-raising
   flour**
2 teaspoons **ground ginger**

To decorate
200 g (7 oz) **plain dark
   chocolate**
200 g (7 oz) **milk chocolate**
12 **white chocolate buttons**

Beat together the butter and sugar until pale and creamy. Add the egg and treacle. Sift the flour and ginger into the bowl and mix all the ingredients to form a firm dough. Knead lightly and chill for 30 minutes.

Grease lightly 2 baking sheets. Roll out the dough to a thickness of 10 cm (½ inch) and cut out heart shapes, using a biscuit cutter. Reroll the trimmings to make more biscuits. Bake in a preheated oven, 180°C (350°F), Gas Mark 4, for about 10 minutes until slightly risen. Transfer to a wire rack and leave to cool.

Melt the plain dark and milk chocolate in separate bowls over pans of simmering water (see page 10). Using a dessertspoon, spoon the plain dark chocolate over about half the biscuits, reserving a little for decoration. Lay a white chocolate button in the centre of half the coated biscuits. Now use the milk chocolate to cover the remaining biscuits, again reserving a little and laying a white chocolate button in the centre of half the coated biscuits.

Put the reserved milk chocolate in a piping bag and with a fine nozzle pipe wavy lines over the biscuits covered with plain dark chocolate. Use the reserved plain dark chocolate to decorate the biscuits covered with milk chocolate. Leave to set.

For iced cinnamon star biscuits, replace the ground ginger with 2 teaspoons ground cinnamon. Roll out as above and stamp out star shapes. To decorate, mix 125 g (4 oz) icing sugar with 2 tablespoons water, drizzle over and top with milk chocolate buttons.

chocolate kisses

Makes **25**
Preparation time **15 minutes**,
  plus cooling and chilling
Cooking time **15 minutes**

2 large **egg whites**
¼ teaspoon **cream of tartar**
225 g (7½ oz) **caster sugar**
4 tablespoons **cocoa powder**,
  sifted
150 g (5 oz) **ground almonds**
1 teaspoon **almond extract**
espresso coffee, to serve

Filling
100 g (3½ oz) **plain dark
  chocolate**, chopped
125 ml (4 fl oz) **double cream**

Whisk the egg whites and cream of tartar in a grease-free bowl until stiff, then gradually whisk in the sugar, 1 tablespoon at a time, until the mixture thickens. Fold in the cocoa powder, almonds and almond extract with a metal spoon until evenly combined.

Spoon the mixture into a piping bag fitted with a large star nozzle and pipe 2.5 cm (1 inch) rosettes onto 2 large, lined baking sheets (you should have 40–50 rosettes, depending on the size).

Bake in a preheated oven, 150°C (300°F), Gas Mark 2, for 15 minutes until the biscuits are just set. Remove from the oven and leave to cool completely on the baking sheets.

Melt the chocolate with the cream in a bowl over a pan of simmering water (see page 10). Cool and then chill for 30 minutes. Whip the chocolate mix until thick and fluffy and use to sandwich the biscuits together to make kisses. Serve with espresso coffee.

For mocha & lemon curd kisses, substitute 2 of the tablespoons cocoa powder with 2 tablespoons ground espresso coffee and fold in as above. Arrange 50 g (2 oz) flaked almonds on top of the piped biscuits before baking as above. Omit the chocolate cream and instead use 5 tablespoons lemon curd mixed with 150 ml (¼ pint) cream as the filling.

mini chocolate logs

Makes **6**
Preparation time **20 minutes**
Cooking time **10 minutes**

3 **eggs**
125 g (4 oz) **golden caster sugar**, plus 2 tablespoons for sprinkling
100 g (3½ oz) **plain flour**
25 g (1 oz) **cocoa powder**
1 tablespoon **hot water**
6 tablespoons ready-made **chocolate spread** or homemade **Chocolate Hazelnut Spread** (see page 128)

Whisk the eggs with the sugar for 10 minutes until they are thick. Sift over the flour and cocoa powder and gently fold them in, along with the measured hot water.

Grease a 33 x 23 cm (13 x 9 inch) Swiss roll tin and line with nonstick baking paper. Pour the mixture into the tin and bake in a preheated oven, 220°C (425°F), Gas Mark 7, for 8–10 minutes until risen and just firm.

Sprinkle a large sheet of nonstick baking paper with sugar. Upturn the cake on to the paper. Carefully peel off the lining paper. Use a sharp knife to trim off all the crisp edges.

Cut the cake in half, to make 2 long strips, then cut each of these strips into 3 pieces. As you cut the cake, cut the nonstick baking paper underneath as well and use a ruler to make sure all the strips are an equal width. Spread each piece of cake with 1 tablespoon chocolate spread. Roll up each cake and remove the baking paper.

For vanilla & chocolate mini logs, whisk the eggs and the sugar with 1 teaspoon vanilla extract, then fold in the flour, 25 g (1 oz) cornflour (in place of the cocoa powder) and the hot water. Bake, trim, fill with chocolate spread and roll up the cake as described above. To decorate, melt 75 g (3 oz) white chocolate in a bowl over a pan of simmering water and drizzle over the finished mini logs.

chocolate cupcakes

Makes **12**
Preparation time **10 minutes**,
 plus cooling
Cooking time **18–20 minutes**
Decoration time **20 minutes**

150 g (5 oz) **butter** or
 margarine
150 g (5 oz) **caster sugar**
175 g (6 oz) **self-raising flour**
3 **eggs**
1 teaspoon **vanilla extract**

To decorate
100 g (3½ oz) **white
 chocolate**, chopped
100 g (3½ oz) **milk chocolate**,
 chopped
100 g (3½ oz) **plain dark
 chocolate**, chopped
40 g (1½ oz) **butter**
cocoa powder, for dusting

Whisk the butter or margarine, sugar, flour, eggs and vanilla extract in a mixing bowl until light and creamy.

Line a 12-section cake baking sheet with paper cases. Divide the mixture evenly among the cases and bake in a preheated oven, 180°C (350°F), Gas Mark 4, for 18–20 minutes until risen and just firm to the touch. Transfer to a wire rack to cool.

Melt the white, milk and plain dark chocolate in 3 separate bowls, each with one-third of the butter added, over pans of simmering water (see page 10). Spread the melted white chocolate over 4 of the cakes and dust with a little cocoa powder.

Put 2 tablespoons each of the melted milk chocolate and plain dark chocolate in separate piping bags fitted with writing nozzles. Spread the milk chocolate over 4 more of the cakes and pipe dots of plain dark chocolate over the milk chocolate. Spread the plain dark chocolate over the 4 remaining cakes and scribble with lines of piped milk chocolate.

For triple chocolate cupcakes, substitute 15 g (½ oz) cocoa powder for 15 g (½ oz) of the self-raising flour and add 50 g (2 oz) chopped white chocolate. Prepare the mixture and bake as above. Decorate the cooled cakes with white chocolate fudge icing made by melting 250 g (8 oz) white chocolate with 125 ml (4 fl oz) single cream and 75 g (3 oz) butter. Cool, then beat until thick and fluffy before piping a large swirl on each cake.

chocolate cigars

Makes **16**
Preparation time **20 minutes**,
   plus setting
Cooking time **4 minutes**
   each batch

1 **egg white**
50 g (2 oz) **caster sugar**
2 tablespoons **plain flour**
1 tablespoon **cocoa powder**
2 tablespoons **double cream**
25 g (1 oz) **butter**, melted
150 g (5 oz) **plain dark**
   chocolate

Whisk the egg white and sugar together until blended. Sift the flour and cocoa powder into the bowl. Stir in the cream and butter.

Line 4 baking sheets with nonstick baking paper. The biscuits will be baked in 4 batches. Place the first 4 dessertspoons, spaced well apart, on a sheet and spread lightly with the back of a spoon. Bake in a preheated oven, 220°C (425°F), Gas Mark 7, for 4 minutes until the biscuits have spread and the edges are beginning to darken.

Remove from the oven and leave for 30 seconds. Using a palette knife, lift each biscuit from the paper and wrap them around the handles of wooden spoons until set. Carefully twist the biscuits off the spoons and transfer them to a wire rack. Bake 3 more batches.

Melt the chocolate in a bowl over a pan of simmering water (see page 10) and dip in 1 side of each biscuit, letting excess chocolate fall back into the bowl. Leave the biscuits on a sheet of nonstick baking paper until they are set.

For white chocolate mousse, to serve with the chocolate cigars, melt 200 g (7 oz) white chocolate and 75 g (3 oz) butter in a bowl over a pan of simmering water. Remove from the heat, then beat in 3 egg yolks, 1 teaspoon vanilla extract and 300 ml (½ pint) whipped double cream. Whisk 3 egg whites and fold into the mixture. Chill to set before serving.

double chocolate cookies

Makes **9**
Preparation time **15 minutes**,
 plus chilling and cooling
Cooking time **10 minutes**

150 g (5 oz) **butter**
150 g (5 oz) **golden caster
 sugar**
1 **egg yolk**
250 g (8 oz) **self-raising
 white flour**
25 g (1 oz) **cocoa powder**
100 g (3½ oz) **plain dark,
 milk or white chocolate**,
 broken into squares

Cream the butter and sugar together until pale and fluffy. Add the egg yolk, then sift in the flour and cocoa powder. Mix together until a firm dough is formed. Knead lightly on a floured surface, wrap and chill for 20 minutes to firm up.

Roll out one-quarter of the dough on a sheet of nonstick baking paper and cut out 9 circles, using a 5 cm (2 inch) cutter. Put a square of chocolate on top of each circle of dough. Roll out another quarter of the remaining dough. Cut out 9 circles again, then use these to sandwich the chocolate squares, pressing the edges well to seal. Transfer the paper and biscuits to a baking sheet. Repeat with the remaining dough.

Bake in a preheated oven, 190°C (375°F), Gas Mark 5, for 10 minutes. Cool for 10 minutes, before transferring to a wire rack.

For ginger & chocolate cookies, omit the cocoa powder and add 1 tablespoon ground ginger and a pinch of ground mixed spice to the biscuit mix, then bake as above. Drain 2 pieces bottled stem ginger, chop and mix with 4 tablespoons good-quality ready-made or homemade chocolate spread (see page 128). When the biscuits are completely cooled, sandwich in pairs with the ginger chocolate spread.

florentines

Makes **48**
Preparation time **30 minutes**,
  plus cooling and setting
Cooking time **40 minutes**

150 g (5 oz) **butter**
175 g (6 oz) **caster sugar**
4 tablespoons **double cream**
75 g (3 oz) **mixed peel**,
  chopped
50 g (2 oz) **glacé cherries**,
  chopped
50 g (2 oz) **flaked almonds**
40 g (1½ oz) **dried**
  cranberries
25 g (1 oz) **pine nuts**
50 g (2 oz) **plain flour**
150 g (5 oz) **plain dark**
  chocolate
150 g (5 oz) **white chocolate**

Heat the butter and sugar gently in a pan until the butter is melted. Increase the heat and bring to the boil. Immediately remove the pan from the heat, add the cream, mixed peel, cherries, almonds, cranberries, pine nuts and flour. Stir well until evenly combined.

Grease 2 large baking sheets and line with nonstick baking paper. Drop 12 heaped teaspoonfuls (a quarter of the mixture) on to each of the baking sheets, leaving a 5 cm (2 inch) gap for spreading. Bake in a preheated oven, 180°C (350°F), Gas Mark 4, for 7 minutes.

Remove the baking sheets from the oven. Using a 7 cm (3 inch) cookie cutter, carefully drag the edges of the biscuits into neat rounds so that they are about 5 cm (2 inches) across. Bake for a further 3–4 minutes until golden around the edges. Remove from the oven and leave for 2 minutes. Use a palette knife to transfer the biscuits to baking paper and leave to cool. Repeat with the remaining mixture.

Melt the plain dark and white chocolate in separate bowls over pans of simmering water (see page 10). Spoon the melted chocolate into separate piping bags and drizzle over the biscuits. Leave to set.

For coconut & chocolate macaroons, whisk 1 large egg white until stiff, then gradually add 225 g (7½ oz) golden caster sugar. Sift over 4 tablespoons plain flour and fold the flour into the mix with 225 g (7½ oz) desiccated coconut. Divide between 2 lined baking sheets, using a 7 cm (3 inch) cookie cutter to cut out 6 rounds on each sheet. Bake as above.

chocolate walnut biscotti

Makes **20**
Preparation time **15 minutes**,
   plus cooling
Cooking time **40 minutes**

200 g (7 oz) **plain dark
   chocolate**
25 g (1 oz) **butter**
200 g (7 oz) **self-raising flour**
1 ½ teaspoons **baking powder**
100 g (3 ½ oz) **light
   muscovado sugar**
50 g (2 oz) **ground semolina**
   or **polenta**
rind of ½ **orange**, finely grated
1 **egg**
1 teaspoon **vanilla essence**
100 g (3 ½ oz) **walnut pieces**
icing sugar, for dusting

Melt the chocolate in a bowl over a pan of simmering water (see page 10), then stir in the butter.

Sift the flour and baking powder into a bowl. Add the sugar, semolina or polenta, orange rind, egg, vanilla essence and walnuts. Add the melted chocolate and butter and mix to form a dough. If the mixture feels dry, add 1 tablespoon water.

Turn the dough out on to a lightly floured surface and divide it in half. Shape each half into a sausage, about 28 cm (11 inches) long. Lightly grease a large baking sheet. Transfer each sausage to the baking sheet and flatten to about 1.5 cm (¾ inch) thick.

Bake in a preheated oven, 160°C (325°F), Gas Mark 3, for 25 minutes or until risen and firm. Leave to cool, then diagonally slice each slab into 1.5 cm (¾ inch) thick biscuits. Return the biscuits to the baking sheet, spacing them slightly apart, and bake for a further 10 minutes until crisp. Leave to cool, then dust with icing sugar.

For chocolate, almond & Brazil nut biscotti, sift 250 g (8 oz) plain flour and 1 ½ teaspoons baking powder into a bowl, then fold in 25 g (1 oz) cocoa powder, 150 g (5 oz) golden caster sugar, 75 g (3 oz) chopped brazil nuts, 3 eggs and 2 teaspoons vanilla extract. Shape into 2 long sausages and bake as above. After cooling and slicing, bake for a further 15 minutes until crisp.

vanilla & cocoa biscuits

Makes **18**
Preparation time **15 minutes**,
  plus chilling and cooling
Cooking time **30 minutes**

125 g (4 oz) **butter**
125 g (4 oz) **golden caster
  sugar**
1 teaspoon **vanilla extract**
175 g (6 oz) **plain flour**
1 tablespoon **cocoa powder**
1 large **egg**
1 **egg yolk**

Icing
125 g (4 oz) **icing sugar**
2 tablespoons **water**

Blend the butter, sugar and vanilla extract in a food processor. Add the flour, cocoa powder, whole egg and yolk. Blend again until the mixture forms a ball. Knead the dough lightly until it is smooth. Wrap and chill for 30 minutes.

Roll out the dough between 2 sheets of baking paper until it is 2.5 mm (⅛ inch) thick. Cut out 15 hearts using a 5 cm (2 inch) cutter. Reroll the trimmings and cut out 3 more heart shapes. Leave the hearts on the baking paper and slide the paper on to 2 firm baking sheets.

Bake in a preheated oven, 180°C (350°F), Gas Mark 4, for 10–12 minutes until the biscuits are firm and golden. Cool for 5 minutes, then transfer to a wire rack to cool completely.

Sift the icing sugar into a bowl, add 1 tablespoon cold water, stir and add another 1 tablespoon water to make a smooth piping consistency. Put into a piping bag with a fine plain nozzle and pipe various designs around the edges of the cookies.

For chocolate-studded honey biscuits, melt 50 g (2 oz) butter in a pan with 2 tablespoons honey and 50 g (2 oz) light soft brown sugar. Tip into a bowl and mix with 50 g (2 oz) plain flour, ½ teaspoon vanilla extract and 2 egg whites. Spoon tablespoons of the mixture on to 2 lined baking sheets and sprinkle with 50 g (2 oz) each chopped dark chocolate and chopped pecans. Bake and finish as above.

tiffin

Serves **8**
Preparation time **30 minutes**,
  plus chilling
Cooking time **5 minutes**

50 g (2 oz) **sultanas**
75 g (3 oz) **dates**, chopped
4 tablespoons **rum**
200 g (7 oz) **plain dark
  chocolate**
125 g (4 oz) **butter**
150 g (5 oz) **golden syrup**
250 g (8 oz) **digestive
  biscuits**, roughly crushed
rind of ½ **orange**, finely grated

Topping
100 g (3½ oz) **plain dark
  chocolate**
100 g (3½ oz) **white
  chocolate**
50 g (2 oz) **Maltesers**,
  chopped

Place the sultanas, dates and rum in a bowl and leave to soak for 30 minutes.

Melt the chocolate, butter and golden syrup together in a pan. Remove from the heat, stir in the biscuits, orange rind and soaked fruit.

Grease an 18 cm (7 inch) square cake tin and line the base. Turn the mixture into the tin and chill for 1 hour.

Melt the plain dark and white chocolate for the topping in 2 separate bowls over pans of simmering water (see page 10). Pour the melted plain dark chocolate on top of the biscuit base, then drizzle over the white chocolate. Drag a cocktail stick through the chocolates to make a swirled effect. Sprinkle over the chopped Maltesers. Chill for at least 2 hours, then cut into wedges to serve.

For milk chocolate, raisin & prune tiffin, omit the sultanas and dates and instead use 50 g (2 oz) raisins and 75 g (3 oz) chopped vanilla prunes. Leave to soak for 30 minutes in 4 tablespoons sherry or brandy. Melt 125 g (4 oz) milk chocolate squares with the butter and golden syrup and continue as above. For the topping, melt 150 g (5 oz) milk chocolate in a bowl over a pan of simmering water and pour on to the biscuit base. Chill and serve as above.

gluten-free choc chip cookies

Makes **30**
Preparation time **10 minutes,**
    plus cooling
Cooking time **10 minutes**

75 g (3 oz) **butter**
100 g (3½ oz) **golden caster
    sugar**
75 g (3 oz) **soft light brown
    sugar**
1 **egg,** beaten
150 g (5 oz) **brown rice flour,**
    plus extra for dusting
½ teaspoon **bicarbonate of
    soda**
1 tablespoon **cocoa powder**
75 g (3 oz) **plain dark
    chocolate chips**

Whiz all the ingredients except the chocolate chips
in a food processor until smooth, or beat in a large
bowl. Stir in the chocolate chips, and bring the mixture
together with your hands to form a ball.

Dust a surface lightly with rice flour. On this, divide
the mixture into 30 balls, then place them, well spaced
apart, on lined baking sheets. Press them down gently
with the back of a fork.

Bake in a preheated oven, 180°C (350°F), Gas Mark
4, for 8–10 minutes. Remove the cookies from the
oven, leave for a few minutes to harden, then transfer
to a wire rack to cool.

For gluten-free cherry & chocolate cookies, use
100 g (3½ oz) light muscovado sugar instead of the
caster sugar and whiz in a processor with the other
ingredients. Stir in 50 g (2 oz) gluten-free chocolate
chips and 50 g (2 oz) dried sour cherries, then
proceed as above.

real chocolate brownies

Makes **10**
Preparation time **15 minutes**,
  plus cooling
Cooking time **25 minutes**

75 g (3 oz) **plain dark
  chocolate**
75 g (3 oz) **butter**
2 **eggs**
250 g (8 oz) **golden caster
  sugar**
100 g (3½ oz) **plain flour**
½ teaspoon **baking powder**

Melt the chocolate with the butter in a bowl over a pan of simmering water (see page 10).

Whisk the eggs and sugar together in a bowl until the mixture is pale and creamy. Stir the melted chocolate into the egg mixture. Sieve in the flour and baking powder and fold together.

Grease a 20 cm (8 inch) square tin and line the base with nonstick baking paper. Turn the mixture into the tin and bake in a preheated oven, 190°C (375°F), Gas Mark 5, for 25 minutes until the brownies are firm on top and a skewer inserted into the centre comes out clean. Cool in the tin for 5 minutes, then them cut into squares.

For toffee, chocolate & nut brownies, add 125 g (4 oz) chopped walnuts, pecans and hazelnuts with the flour. Melt 200 g (7 oz) creamy toffees with 4 tablespoons double cream. Spread half the brownie mixture in the prepared tin. Pour over the toffee sauce, then spread over the rest of the brownie mixture. Bake as above.

pine nut caramel slices

Makes **12**

Preparation time **20 minutes**,
   plus chilling and cooling

Cooking time **20–25 minutes**

125 g (4 oz) **butter**
65 g (2½ oz) **caster sugar**,
   plus extra for dusting
125 g (4 oz) **plain flour**
65 g (2½ oz) **rice flour**
pinch of **salt**
200 g (7 oz) **plain dark
   chocolate**

Pine nut caramel
50 g (2 oz) **butter**
50 g (2 oz) **soft brown sugar**
400 g (13 oz) **sweetened
   condensed milk**
50 g (2 oz) **pine nuts**

Whisk the butter and sugar in a bowl until pale and light. Sift in the flour, rice flour and salt and work the ingredients together to form a soft dough. Shape the dough into a flat disc, wrap in clingfilm and chill for 30 minutes.

Grease and line a 20 cm (8 inch) square baking tin with baking paper, allowing the paper to overhang the sides of the tin. Roll out the dough on a lightly floured surface and press into the prepared tin, smoothing it as flat as possible. Bake in a preheated oven, 190°C (375°F), Gas Mark 5, for 20–25 minutes until golden. Remove from the oven and leave to cool in the tin.

Heat the butter, sugar and condensed milk gently in a pan, stirring constantly until the butter has melted and the sugar has completely dissolved. Increase the heat and bring to the boil, whisking constantly for up to 5 minutes until the mixture thickens. Remove from the heat, stir in the pine nuts and pour the caramel mixture over the shortbread layer. Leave until set. Chill for 2 hours until firm.

Melt the chocolate in a bowl over a pan of simmering water (see page 10). Pour over the caramel layer and spread flat with a palette knife. Leave to set. Once set, remove from the tin and cut into 12 slices.

For white chocolate & caramel pine nut slices, substitute 65 g (2½ oz) cornflour for the rice flour and combine with the other ingredients as above. When making the topping, use 200 g (7 oz) white chocolate instead of the plain dark chocolate and add a drop of vanilla extract.

chocolate macaroons

Makes **25**
Preparation time **10 minutes**
Cooking time **15 minutes**

50 g (2 oz) **plain dark
    chocolate**, grated
2 **egg whites**
100 g (3½ oz) **caster sugar**
125 g (4 oz) **ground almonds**
25 **chocolate coffee beans**,
    to decorate

Whisk the egg whites until stiff. Gradually whisk in the sugar until the mixture is thick and glossy. Gently fold in the ground almonds and grated chocolate.

Line a large baking sheet with nonstick baking paper. Put the mixture in a piping bag fitted with a large plain nozzle and pipe small rounds, about 4 cm (1½ inches) in diameter, on to the baking sheet. Alternatively, place small teaspoonfuls on the baking sheet.

Press a chocolate coffee bean into the centre of each macaroon. Bake in a preheated oven, 180°C (350°F), Gas Mark 4, for about 15 minutes until slightly risen and just firm. Leave the macaroons on the baking paper to cool.

For white chocolate & pistachio macaroons, replace the plain dark chocolate with 50 g (2 oz) white chocolate. Grind 125 g (4 oz) pistachios in a food processor and use in place of the almonds. Otherwise, prepare and bake as above.

twists on classics

chocolate brownie fudge trifle

Serves **10**

Preparation time **30 minutes**, plus chilling

Cooking time **10 minutes**

200 g (7 oz) ready-made **chocolate brownies** or **Real Chocolate Brownies** (see page 192)

3 tablespoons **chocolate liqueur**

225 g (7½ oz) **plain dark chocolate**

225 ml (7½ fl oz) **boiling water**

20 **Belgian chocolate thins**, to decorate

Custard

3 **egg yolks**

25 g (1 oz) **golden caster sugar**

1 teaspoon **cornflour**

275 ml (9 fl oz) **double cream**

Topping

275 ml (9 fl oz) **double cream**

1 teaspoon **vanilla extract**

1 tablespoon **maple syrup**

Break up the chocolate brownies and arrange them at the base of 10 individual glass dishes. Drizzle over the chocolate liqueur.

Melt the chocolate in a bowl over a pan of simmering water (see page 10). Add the measured boiling water 1 tablespoon at a time, stirring well between each addition to make a smooth sauce. Pour the sauce over the brownies, cover and chill for 2 hours.

Mix the egg yolks, sugar and cornflour for the custard in a jug. Bring the cream to the boil in a pan, then pour it over the egg mixture, whisking all the time. Return the custard to the pan and heat gently, stirring all the time, until the sauce is thickened and smooth. Pour the custard into a jug and cover with nonstick baking paper. Chill for 1 hour. Once the chocolate layer has set, pour the custard over and chill.

Whip the cream until softly peaking, then fold in the vanilla extract and maple syrup. Spoon the cream on top of the custard. Decorate with the chocolate thins.

For banoffee brownie trifles, chill the brownies in chocolate sauce as above. Combine 2 sliced bananas with 6 tablespoons tropical fruit juice and spoon over the chocolate sauce layer. Mix 250 ml (8 fl oz) ready-made or homemade custard with 250 g (8 oz) mascarpone cheese. Spoon on top of the banana layer and drizzle with 4 tablespoons dulce de leche (toffee caramel).

chocolate baked alaska

Serves **4–6**
Preparation time **10 minutes**,
plus freezing
Cooking time **5 minutes**

1 small **sponge flan case**
2 tablespoons **apple juice** or
chocolate liqueur
4 tablespoons **cherry,
raspberry or strawberry
jam**
500 ml (17 fl oz) tall tub
luxury chocolate ice cream
3 **egg whites**
125 g (4 oz) **golden caster
sugar**

Place the sponge flan case in an ovenproof pie dish.
Drizzle over the apple juice or chocolate liqueur, then
spoon on the jam and spread it over evenly.

Run a blunt knife around the sides of the ice cream
to help loosen it from the tub. Upturn the ice cream on
top of the sponge flan case. Place on a flat surface in
the freezer.

Whisk the egg whites in a grease-free bowl (if you
see any yolk, remove it with a teaspoon) until they turn
white and thick. Lift up the bowl and tip it slightly from
side to side; if they don't move, they are ready. Whisk
in 1 tablespoon of the sugar at a time until the
meringue is smooth, glossy and stiffly peaking.

Spread the meringue over the prepared ice cream
base using a palette knife, making sure the ice cream
is completely covered and the meringue seals the edge
of the sponge flan case. Return to the freezer for at
least 1 hour (you can leave it for up to a day).

Bake in a preheated oven, 220°C (425°F), Gas Mark 7,
for 5 minutes until the meringue is just starting to get
tinged with brown, then serve immediately.

For double chocolate baked alaskas, arrange
6 chocolate brownies (see page 192) in the base of
an ovenproof flan dish and use instead of the sponge
flan case. Add 100 g (3½ oz) white chocolate chips
to the meringue mixture and proceed as above.

flourless chocolate cake

Serves **8**

Preparation time **1–2 minutes**, plus cooling

Cooking time **50 minutes**

300 g (10 oz) **plain dark chocolate**, broken into pieces

175 g (6 oz) **butter**

2 teaspoons **vanilla extract**

5 **eggs**

6 tablespoons **thick double cream**, plus extra to serve (optional)

225 g (7½ oz) **golden caster sugar**

handful of **blueberries**

handful of **raspberries**

Melt the chocolate and butter together in a large bowl over a pan of simmering water (see page 10), stirring until the mixture is smooth. Remove from the heat and add the vanilla extract.

Beat the eggs, cream and golden caster sugar for 3–4 minutes (the mixture will remain fairly runny), then fold into the chocolate mixture.

Line the base and sides of a 23 cm (9 inch) cake tin with nonstick baking paper. Pour the mixture into the tin and bake in a preheated oven, 180°C (350°F), Gas Mark 4, for 45 minutes, or until the top forms a crust. Allow the cake to cool and then run a knife around the edges to loosen it from the tin.

Turn out the cake on to a serving plate and top with a mixture of blueberries and raspberries. Serve with extra cream, if desired.

For fresh strawberry coulis, to accompany the cake instead of the fruit and cream, whiz 200 g (7 oz) fresh raspberries with 2 tablespoons golden caster sugar in a processor until smooth. Press through a metal sieve before serving around slices of the cake.

white chocolate & vanilla muffins

Makes **12**
Preparation time **15 minutes**,
  plus cooling
Cooking time **25 minutes**

125 g (4 oz) **plain flour**
200 g (7 oz) **self-raising flour**
½ teaspoon **baking powder**
125 g (4 oz) **white chocolate**,
  coarsely grated or chopped
½ teaspoon **bicarbonate of
  soda**
200 g (7 oz) **golden caster
  sugar**
rind of **1 lemon**, finely grated
200 g (7 oz) **butter**, melted
3 large **eggs**
125 ml (4 fl oz) **soured cream**
1 teaspoon **vanilla extract**
125 ml (4 fl oz) **sweet
  dessert wine**
icing sugar, for dusting

Sift both flours and the baking powder into a large bowl. Add the white chocolate, bicarbonate of soda, sugar and lemon rind and mix everything together.

Mix together the butter, eggs, cream and vanilla extract in a large jug. Pour the wet ingredients on to the dry ingredients and stir together to combine.

Line a 12-hole muffin tin with paper muffin cases. Spoon the mixture into the cases and bake in a preheated oven, 180°C (350°F), Gas Mark 4, for 25 minutes until risen, firm, pale golden and a cocktail stick comes out clean when it is inserted into the centre of a muffin.

Loosen the muffins with a palette knife and cool on a wire rack. Pierce the muffins several times with a cocktail stick and pour over the sweet wine. Dust with icing sugar to serve.

For special muffin topping, melt 200 g (7 oz) white chocolate with a 140 g (4½ oz) jar liquid glucose. Mix in 100 g (3½ oz) sieved golden icing sugar and stir to form a ball. Cut into 12 pieces, mould into twirled flower shapes and place one on top of each muffin. Decorate the muffins no more than a few hours before serving.

white chocolate fruit cake

Serves **35**
Preparation time **1½ hours**,
  plus cooling
Cooking time **2 hours**

625 g (1¼ lb) **mixed dried
  fruit**
150 ml (¼ pint) **brandy**
500 g (1 lb) **butter**
500 g (1 lb) **muscovado
  sugar**
8 **eggs**
500g (1 lb) **self-raising flour**
50g (2 oz) **cocoa powder**
1 tablespoon **ground mixed
  spice**
1 tablespoon **ground ginger**
200 g (7 oz) **pecan nuts**
200 g (7 oz) **milk chocolate**
200 g (7 oz) **white chocolate**,
  chopped
6 tablespoons ready-made
  apricot glaze (or use
  warmed, sieved **apricot jam**)
1k g (2 lb) **white marzipan**

To decorate
cabbage roses or
  white roses
golden icing sugar

Warm the dried fruit gently in a pan with two-thirds of
the brandy.

Cream together the butter and sugar until fluffy.
Gradually whisk in the eggs. Sift in the flour, cocoa
powder, mixed spiced and ginger. Stir in the nuts,
milk and white chocolate, soaked fruit and liquid. Mix
to combine.

Grease and line a 23 cm (9 inch) round cake tin and a
15 cm (6 inch) round cake tin. Turn the mixture into the
tins and bake in a preheated oven, 150°C (300°F), Gas
Mark 2, for 1¾ hours for the small cake and 2 hours
for the large one. Cool the cakes in the tins.

Warm the apricot glaze with the rest of the brandy.
Slice the top off the large cake to level it. Place on
a plate and brush all over with the apricot glaze.

Roll out two-thirds of the marzipan, on a surface
dusted with icing sugar, to a 33 cm (13 inch) circle.
Use to cover the large cake and trim off the excess.
Top with the smaller cake and brush it with the apricot
glaze. Roll the rest of the marzipan to a 25 cm (10 inch)
circle and use it to cover the small cake.

Tie a wide ribbon around both cakes and decorate with
roses. Dust with icing sugar to finish.

For white chocolate cake covering, melt 800 g (1 lb
10 oz) white chocolate with 560 g (1lb 2½ oz) liquid
glucose. Remove from the heat, add 400 g (13 oz)
sieved golden icing sugar and stir to a ball. Roll out
two-thirds to cover the large cake and the rest for the
small cake. Use trimmings to mould rose decorations.

choc, fruit & nut cake

Serves **12**
Preparation time **15 minutes**,
   plus cooling
Cooking time **about 2 hours**

3 **flaky chocolate bars**,
   chopped into 1.5 cm
   (¾ inch) pieces
225 g (7½ oz) **butter** or
   margarine
225 g (7½ oz) **caster sugar**
275 g (9 oz) **self-raising flour**
25 g (1 oz) **cocoa powder**
4 **eggs**
150 g (5 oz) **hazelnuts**,
   roughly chopped
200 g (7 oz) **plain dark
   chocolate**, chopped
225 g (7½ oz) **raisins**
cocoa powder or **icing sugar**,
   for dusting

Cream together the butter or margarine and sugar.
Add the flour, cocoa powder and eggs to the bowl
and beat until smooth. Reserve half the pieces of flaky
chocolate and 50 g (2 oz) each of the hazelnuts and
plain dark chocolate. Fold the remainder into the cake
mixture with the raisins.

Grease and line a 20 cm (8 inch) round or 18 cm
(7 inch) square cake tin. Turn the mixture into the tin
and scatter with the reserved chocolate and nuts. Bake
in a preheated oven, 150°C (300°F), Gas Mark 2, for
about 2 hours or until a skewer inserted into the centre
comes out clean.

Leave to cool in the tin. Serve lightly dusted with
cocoa powder or icing sugar.

For chocolate, banana & almond traybake, prepare
the cake mixture as above, but replace 75 g (3 oz)
of the flour with 75 g (3 oz) ground almonds and
the 50 g (2 oz) hazelnuts with 50 g (2 oz) flaked
almonds. Stir in 2 ripe mashed bananas. Turn the
mixture into a prepared 18 x 28 cm (7 x 11 inch)
rectangular tin and sprinkle with the reserved
chocolate and 100 g (3½ oz) flaked almonds instead
of the hazelnuts. Bake as above and cut into squares
to serve.

chocolate mince pies

Makes **12**
Preparation time **45 minutes**,
   plus chilling and cooling
Cooking time **30 minutes**

350 g (11½ oz) **plain flour**,
   plus extra for dusting
3 tablespoons **cocoa powder**
6 tablespoons **icing sugar**
200 g (7 oz) **butter**, chilled
   and cubed
1 large **egg**, lightly beaten
1–2 tablespoons **ice-cold
   water**
750 g (1½ lb) **mincemeat**
75 g (3 oz) **pecan nuts**,
   chopped
50 g (2 oz) **plain dark
   chocolate**, chopped
3 tablespoons **apricot glaze**
   or **cranberry jelly**
1 tablespoon **golden icing
   sugar**, for dusting

Whiz the flour, cocoa powder and icing sugar together in a food processor for a few seconds. Add the butter and blend to form crumbs, then pour in the egg and 1 tablespoon water, and pulse until the mixture begins to come together (add more water if necessary). Knead the pastry until smooth on a lightly floured surface. Wrap in clingfilm and chill for 1 hour.

Roll out the pastry on a lightly floured surface. Using a 12 cm (5 inch) tartlet tin or saucer as a guide, cut out circles. Knead the trimmings together gently, re-roll the pastry and cut out some more circles.

Grease a 12-hole deep muffin tin (not a regular patty tin) or line with paper muffin cases. Ease the pastry circles into the tins and chill for 15 minutes. Spoon in the mincemeat and sprinkle over the pecan and chocolate pieces.

Press the pastry edges up and over the filling to make a rim. Brush the tops with apricot glaze or cranberry jelly and bake in a preheated oven, 200°C (400°F), Gas Mark 6, for 30 minutes. Cool in the tin. Remove from the tin and cases and dust with icing sugar to serve.

For almond streusel topping, mix together 50 g (2 oz) each of flaked almonds, demerara sugar and crushed digestives and sprinkle over the top of the mincemeat instead of the chocolate pecan topping.

toffee choux buns

Makes **8**

Preparation time **30 minutes**, plus cooling

Cooking time **45 minutes**

50 g (2 oz) **butter**

150 ml (¼ pint) **sparkling spring water**

1 tablespoon **golden caster sugar**

65 g (2½ oz) **plain flour**, sifted on to a piece of nonstick baking paper

2 **eggs**, lightly beaten

Topping

200 g (7 oz) **plain dark chocolate**

75 g (3 oz) **butter**

Filling

300 ml (½ pint) **double cream**

1 teaspoon **vanilla extract**

1 teaspoon **golden caster sugar**

8 tablespoons **dulce de leche** (toffee caramel)

Melt the butter with the spring water and sugar in a heavy-based pan. Bring to the boil, turn off the heat and immediately tip in all the flour. Beat vigorously with a wooden spoon until the mixture forms a ball in the centre of the pan. Tip the ball into a bowl and cool for 15 minutes. Whisk in the eggs gradually until the mixture is smooth and glossy.

Sprinkle water over a nonstick baking sheet. Put 8 large spoonfuls of the mixture, well spaced apart, on to the baking sheet. Bake in a preheated oven, 220°C (425°F), Gas Mark 7, for 30 minutes until risen and golden brown, then turn off the oven. Pierce each bun with a sharp knife to let the steam escape and leave in the oven for 10–15 minutes to dry out. Transfer to a wire rack and cool completely.

Melt the chocolate with the butter in a bowl over a pan of simmering water (see page 10), to make the topping. Use a serrated knife to cut the choux buns in half.

Whip the cream with the vanilla extract and sugar. Spread a spoonful of dulce de leche (toffee caramel) into the base of each bun and top with a spoonful of whipped cream and the choux bun lids. Spoon the melted chocolate on top.

For banoffee toffee choux buns, slice 2 small bananas and toss the slices in 2 teaspoons lemon juice. Put a few banana slices on top of the caramel layer in the middle of each of the choux buns.

214

choc, orange & oatmeal muffins

Makes **9–10**
Preparation time **10 minutes**
Cooking time **15–20 minutes**

225 g (7½ oz) **plain flour**
2 teaspoons **baking powder**
rind of **1 orange**, finely grated
50 g (2 oz) **medium oatmeal**,
  plus extra for sprinkling
75 g (3 oz) **light muscovado
  sugar**
200 g (7 oz) **Greek yogurt**
4 tablespoons **sunflower or
  vegetable oil**
150 ml (¼ pint) **milk**
1 **egg**
200 g (7 oz) **milk chocolate**,
  chopped

Sift the flour and baking powder into a bowl. Stir in the orange rind, oatmeal and sugar.

Beat the yogurt with the oil, milk and egg and add to the bowl of dry ingredients with the chocolate. Using a large metal spoon, carefully fold the ingredients together until only just combined, adding a little extra milk if the mixture seems dry.

Line a 10-section deep bun tin or muffin tin with paper muffin cases. Divide the mixture among the cases and sprinkle some extra oatmeal over the top. Bake the muffins in a preheated oven, 200°C (400°F), Gas Mark 6, for 15–20 minutes until risen and just firm. Serve warm or cold.

For breakfast muesli muffins, substitute 75 g (3 oz) muesli for the oatmeal and combine with the dry ingredients as above. Add in the yogurt, oil, milk and egg with a reduced quantity of 75 g (3 oz) chopped milk chocolate, then fold in and bake as above.

fruity chocolate flapjacks

Makes **12**

Preparation time **20 minutes**,
  plus cooling and setting

Cooking time **25–30 minutes**

200 g (7 oz) **butter**
150 g (5 oz) **golden syrup**
450 g (14½ oz) **rolled oats**
75 g (3 oz) **light muscovado
  sugar**
125 g (4 oz) **mixed dried fruit**
  (such as cranberries, sour
  cherries, blueberries)
200 g (7 oz) **milk chocolate**

Melt the butter and golden syrup in a pan over a low heat. Remove from the heat and mix in the oats, sugar and fruit. Stir everything together.

Grease a 23 cm (9 inch) square and 6 cm (2½ inch) deep tin. Turn the mixture into the tin and press down with the back of a spoon. Bake in a preheated oven, 190°C (375°F), Gas Mark 5, for 25–30 minutes until golden and firm. Cool.

Melt the chocolate in a bowl over a pan of simmering water (see page 10) and pour it over the flapjack mixture. Leave to cool and set. Cut into 12 slices.

For tropical fruit & white chocolate flapjacks, use 125 g (4 oz) chopped dried mango, papaya and pineapple instead of the dried fruits and bake as above. Instead of a milk chocolate topping, melt 200 g (7 oz) white chocolate, pour it over the flapjack mixture, then sprinkle with 3 tablespoons sweetened tenderized desiccated coconut.

chocolate, maple & pecan tart

Serves **8**

Preparation time **30 minutes**, plus cooling

Cooking time **35–40 minutes**

200 g (7 oz) **plain dark chocolate**

50 g (2 oz) **butter**

75 g (3 oz) **caster sugar**

175 ml (6 fl oz) **maple syrup**

3 **eggs**

350 g (11½ oz) **puff pastry** or **dessert shortcrust pastry**, thawed if frozen

125 g (4 oz) **pecan nuts**

icing sugar, for dusting

Preheat the oven to 180°C (350°F), Gas Mark 4, and put a baking sheet in the oven to heat through. Melt the chocolate in a bowl over a pan of simmering water (see page 10) and stir in the butter.

Heat the sugar and maple syrup in a pan gently until the sugar dissolves. Leave to cool slightly. Lightly whisk the eggs to a smooth consistency. Whisk in both the chocolate and the syrup mixtures.

Grease a loose-based flan tin, 23 cm (9 inches) in diameter and 3 cm (1¼ inches) deep. Roll out the pastry on a lightly floured surface and use to line the tin. Pour the filling into the pastry case. Place on the hot baking sheet in the oven and bake for 15 minutes until the filling is just beginning to set.

Remove the tart from the oven and scatter the pecan nuts over the top. Bake for a further 10 minutes until the nuts are beginning to brown. Remove from the oven and raise the temperature to 230°C (450°F), Gas Mark 8. Dust the tart generously with icing sugar and return to the oven for about 5 minutes until the nuts are beginning to caramelize. Leave to cool for 20 minutes before serving.

For chocolate, honey & nut tart, replace the dark chocolate with 100 g (3½ oz) each of milk chocolate and plain dark chocolate. Replace the maple syrup with 175 ml (6 fl oz) runny honey. Scatter the tart with 75 g (3 oz) pine nuts and 50 g (2 oz) pistachio nuts instead of the pecans and bake as above.

christmas pudding parfait

Serves **12**

Preparation time **30 minutes**, plus freezing

Cooking time **5 minutes**

finely grated rind and juice of **1 orange**

2 tablespoons **Southern Comfort** or **sherry**, plus 12 teaspoons to serve

125 g (4 oz) **raisins**

125 g (4 oz) ready-to-eat **vanilla prunes**, chopped

1 teaspoon **ground mixed spice**

125 g (4 oz) **dark muscovado sugar**, plus 1 tablespoon extra

4 large **eggs**, separated

575 ml (18 fl oz) **double cream**, whipped until softly peaking

125 g (4 oz) **plain dark chocolate flavoured with orange and spices**, grated

Heat the orange rind and juice and Southern Comfort or sherry gently in a pan with the raisins, prunes and mixed spice for 3–5 minutes until the fruit has plumped up and the liquid has been absorbed. Purée in a food processor.

Beat 125 g (4 oz) sugar and the egg yolks together in a bowl for 5 minutes until thick and creamy. Fold in the cream. Add the blended fruit and chocolate.

Whisk the egg whites in a grease-free bowl until softly peaking. Whisk in the extra 1 tablespoon sugar. Fold the egg whites into the rest of the mixture and gently mix together.

Line a 1 kg (2 lb) loaf tin with clingfilm. Freeze the mixture in the tin for 6 hours. Serve sliced on large plates drizzled with 1 teaspoon Southern Comfort or sherry around each slice.

For butterscotch sauce, to serve with the parfait, mix 50 g (2 oz) butter, 50 g (2 oz) golden caster sugar, 75 g (3 oz) light muscovado sugar and 150 g (5 oz) golden syrup in a pan. Heat gently, stirring, until melted and smooth. Continue to cook over a low heat for 5 minutes. Remove from the heat and slowly stir in 125 ml (4 fl oz) double cream, a few drops of vanilla extract and the juice of ½ lemon.

chocolate devil's food cake

Serves **12**
Preparation time **30 minutes**,
  plus cooling
Cooking time **35 minutes**

225 g (7½ oz) **plain flour**
1 teaspoon **bicarbonate of
  soda**
50 g (2 oz) **cocoa powder**
125 g (4 oz) **butter**
250 g (8 oz) **light muscovado
  sugar**
3 **eggs**
250 ml (8 fl oz) **milk**
1 tablespoon **lemon juice**

Frosting
175 g (6 oz) **plain dark
  chocolate**
75 g (3 oz) **milk chocolate**
3 tablespoons **golden caster
  sugar**
300 ml (½ pint) **soured cream**

Sift together the flour, bicarbonate of soda and cocoa powder. Cream together the butter and half the sugar until soft and fluffy. Gradually whisk in the eggs, then whisk in the rest of the sugar. Mix the milk with the lemon juice to sour it, then fold into the flour mixture until smoothly combined.

Grease 2 cake tins, 20 cm (8 inch) in diameter, and line the bases with nonstick baking paper. Spoon the mixture equally into the prepared tins and level over the surface of both.

Bake in a preheated oven, 180°C (350°F), Gas Mark 4, for 30 minutes until risen, springy to the touch and shrinking away from the edges of the tin. Cool in the tins for 10 minutes, then upturn the cakes on to a wire rack to cool.

Melt the dark and milk chocolate together in a bowl over a pan of simmering water (see page 10), then remove from the heat and whisk in the sugar and soured cream to make the frosting.

Slice each cake in half horizontally to make 4 layers. Put one layer on the serving dish and spread with one-quarter of the frosting. Top with another cake layer, then some more frosting. Continue layering cake and frosting, ending with frosting on top.

For mascarpone topping, instead of the rich chocolate frosting, mix 500 g (1 lb) mascarpone cheese, 50 g (2 oz) light muscovado sugar, 1 teaspoon vanilla extract and 1 tablespoon chocolate liqueur until smooth, then spread on top of each chocolate cake layer.

chocolate sorbet

Serves **6**
Preparation time **5 minutes**,
  plus cooling, churning and
  freezing
Cooking time **15 minutes**

200 g (7 oz) **dark
  muscovado sugar**
50 g (2 oz) **cocoa powder**
1 teaspoon **instant espresso
  coffee powder**
1 **cinnamon stick**
600 ml (1 pint) **water**
12 **chocolate coffee
  matchsticks**
2 tablespoons **chocolate
  liqueur**, to serve

Mix the sugar, cocoa powder, coffee and cinnamon stick in a large pan with the measured water. Slowly bring to the boil, stirring until the sugar has dissolved, boil for 5 minutes, then take off the heat. Leave to cool. Remove the cinnamon stick.

Pour the cooled liquid into a freezer-proof container, seal and freeze for 2–4 hours until firm. Whiz in a food processor until smooth, then pour into a 1 kg (2 lb) loaf tin and freeze for 2 hours or until frozen solid. Alternatively, place in an ice cream maker and churn for 30 minutes until frozen, then pour into a loaf tin and freeze for 2 hours.

Turn out on to a serving plate and arrange the coffee matchsticks over the top to decorate. Cut into slices to serve and drizzle 1 teaspoon chocolate liqueur around each portion.

For chocolate peppermint sorbet, omit the coffee and cinnamon stick and add 1 teaspoon peppermint extract in the first step. To serve, scoop into balls and place in individual glasses, decorating each glass with a fresh mint spring and serving with 2 or 3 chocolate peppermint matchsticks.

chocolate ripple teabread

Serves **10**
Preparation time **15 minutes**,
   plus cooling
Cooking time 1½ **hours**

200 g (7 oz) **plain dark
   chocolate**
200 g (7 oz) **butter**
1 teaspoon **ground mixed
   spice**
175 g (6 oz) **golden caster
   sugar**
3 **eggs**
2 teaspoons **vanilla extract**
225 g (7½ oz) **self-raising
   flour**
½ teaspoon **baking powder**
100 g (3½ oz) **plain dark
   chocolate**, chopped

Melt the chocolate in a bowl over a pan of simmering water (see page 10) and stir in 25 g (1 oz) of the butter and the mixed spice.

Place the remaining butter, sugar, eggs and vanilla extract in a bowl. Sift the flour and baking powder into the bowl and beat until light and fluffy.

Grease the base and long sides of a 1 kg (2 lb) loaf tin. Spoon one-quarter of the mixture into the tin. Spread one-third of the chocolate mixture over the cake mixture. Repeat the layering of the cake mixture and chocolate sauce, finishing with a layer of cake mixture. Sprinkle with the chopped chocolate.

Bake in a preheated oven, 180°C (350°F), Gas Mark 4, for 1¼ hours or until risen and a skewer inserted into the centre of the teabread comes out clean. Leave in the tin for 10 minutes, then transfer to a wire rack to cool.

For chocolate orange ripple teabread, omit the vanilla extract and instead add the juice and finely grated rind of 2 oranges. Bake as above. When you take the teabread out the oven, immediately drizzle the top with 2 tablespoons warm marmalade to make a sticky glaze.

choc & maple syrup brownies

Makes **12**
Preparation time **15 minutes**,
  plus cooling
Cooking time **35–40 minutes**

275 g (9 oz) **plain dark
  chocolate**
250 g (8 oz) **butter**
3 **eggs**
175 g (6 oz) **caster sugar**
50 ml (2 fl oz) **maple syrup**
100 g (3½ oz) **self-raising
  flour**
pinch **salt**
100 g (3½ oz) **walnuts,**
  toasted and chopped
  (optional)
125 g (4 oz) **white chocolate,**
  chopped
icing sugar, for dusting

Melt the plain dark chocolate and butter together in a bowl over a pan of simmering water (see page 10).

Whisk the eggs with the sugar and maple syrup until pale and light, then stir in the melted chocolate mixture, flour, salt and walnuts, if used.

Grease and line a 30 x 20 cm (12 x 8 inch) baking tin, allowing the paper to overhang the edges of the tin. Spoon the mixture into the tin and scatter the white chocolate over the surface.

Bake in a preheated oven, 190°C (375°F), Gas Mark 5, for 35–40 minutes until the top sets but the cake mix still feels soft underneath. Cover the tin loosely with foil if the surface begins to brown too much. Leave to cool in the tin. Dust with icing sugar and cut into squares to serve.

For chocolate cherry brownies, use 275 g (9 oz) dark chocolate flavoured with cherries instead of the plain dark chocolate. Add 50 g (2 oz) dried sour cherries to the melted chocolate mixture with the other ingredients, then continue as described above.

low-fat chocolate soufflés

Makes **6**
Preparation time **5 minutes**,
  plus cooling
Cooking time **20 minutes**

50 g (2 oz) **plain dark
  chocolate**, broken into
  pieces
2 tablespoons **cornflour**
1 tablespoon **cocoa powder**
1 teaspoon **instant espresso
  granules**
4 tablespoons **golden caster
  sugar**
150 ml (¼ pint) **skimmed
  milk**
2 **eggs**, separated
1 **egg white**
1 tablespoon **cocoa powder**,
  sifted, for dusting

Heat the chocolate, cornflour, cocoa powder and coffee granules with 1 tablespoon of the sugar and the milk in a pan over a low heat until the chocolate has melted. Continue heating, stirring all the time until the chocolate mixture thickens. Remove from the heat and cool slightly, then stir in the egg yolks and cover with a piece of nonstick baking paper.

Whisk all the egg whites in a grease-free bowl until softly peaking. Gradually whisk in the rest of the sugar until the eggs are stiffly peaking. Fold one-third of the egg whites into the chocolate mixture, then fold in the rest of the egg whites.

Grease 6 heatproof cups or ramekins, each 150 ml (¼ pint), and spoon in the chocolate soufflé mixture. Bake in a preheated oven, 190°C (375°F), Gas Mark 5, on a hot baking sheet for 12 minutes or until the soufflés are puffed up.

Dust with cocoa powder and eat immediately.

For chocolate surprise soufflé, prepare the soufflé mixture as described above, omitting the espresso coffee. Half-fill each cup or ramekin, add 1–2 squares milk chocolate to each and top with the rest of the soufflé mixture. Bake as above.

triple chocolate fondue

Serves **8**
Preparation time **15 minutes**
Cooking time **10 minutes**

150 g (5 oz) **plain dark
  chocolate**
150 g (5 oz) **milk chocolate**
150 g (5 oz) **white chocolate**
300 ml (½ pint) **double cream**
75 ml (3 fl oz) **mild olive oil**

For dipping
200 g (7 oz) fresh
  strawberries
200 g (7 oz) fresh
  raspberries
amaretti biscuits

Melt the plain dark, milk and white chocolate in 3 separate bowls over pans of simmering water (see page 10), each with one-third of the cream and one-third of the olive oil.

Pour each chocolate into a separate small bowl or mini fondue pot with a lighted tealight candle underneath.

Serve the chocolate fondues with strawberries, raspberries and amaretti biscuits for dipping.

For children's chocolate fondue, omit the dark chocolate and use 200 g (7 oz) each milk and white chocolate. Serve with 200 g (7 oz) marshmallows threaded on to cocktail sticks with the strawberries and raspberries.

index

acknowledgements

Executive editor: Nicky Hill
Editor: Fiona Robertson
Executive Art Editor: Sally Bond
Designer: Geoff Borin
Photographer: David Munns
Food stylist: Felicity Barnum-Bobb
Prop stylist: Liz Hippisley
Senior Production Controller: Manjit Sihra

Special photography: © Octopus Publishing Group Limited/David Munns
Other photography: © Octopus Publishing Group Limited/Stephen Conroy 161; /Gus Filgate 85; /Jeremy Hopley 61; /David Loftus 77; /Lis Parsons 83, 87, 165; /Emma Neish 155, 191; /Gareth Sambridge 177; /Ian Wallace 38, 43, 51, 57, 67, 81, 95, 103, 107, 121, 123, 143, 153, 171, 172, 179, 185, 194, 197, 211, 217, 221, 228, 231.